INCEST

THE SILENT SIN

Incest is taboo in almost every society. Yet it is a taboo that is broken more often than most of us dare admit. The effects of *incest* are always tragic—crippling guilt that manifests itself in a long list of extreme psychological disturbances.

The Silent Sin is an intensely intimate story of an incestuous relationship—of a father and daughter who were lovers.

MENTOR and SIGNET Titles of Special Interest

☐ **SOMEWHERE A CHILD IS CRYING: Maltreatment—Causes and Prevention by Vincent J. Fontana, M.D.** A compelling and compassionate account of the battered child syndrome . . . "Like taking a walk through hell . . . should be universally required reading."—*Publishers Weekly* (#ME1663—$2.25)

☐ **SOUL MURDER: Persecution in the Family by Dr. Morton Schatzman.** A bizarre and frightening case of mental illness in which a son was driven mad by his own father. A devastating indictment of the system of inhuman child-rearing that shaped the society that produced Hitler . . . "An enthralling psychiatric detective story!" —*Newsweek* (#ME1499—$1.75)

☐ **DAUGHTERS AND MOTHERS: MOTHERS AND DAUGHTERS by Signe Hammer.** Here is a book that can help you understand how the bond between mother and daughter can enable the daughter to become a strong, "free" woman or keep her tied to her mother in a mutually dependent relationship that allows neither of them to grow. (#W7218—$1.50)

☐ **LOVECHILD by Mary Hanes.** An unwed mother's triumph over loneliness and despair—a story suffused with love and a poignant affirmation of life. (#W7260—$1.50)

☐ **AUTOBIOGRAPHY OF A SCHIZOPHRENIC GIRL with analytic interpretation by Marguerite Sechehaye.** The astonishing personal story of a flight into madness—and of the difficult path back. (#Y7812—$1.25)

THE NEW AMERICAN LIBRARY, INC.,
P.O. Box 999, Bergenfield, New Jersey 07621

Please send me the MENTOR and SIGNET BOOKS I have checked above. I am enclosing $_____ (check or money order—no currency or C.O.D.'s). Please include the list price plus 35¢ a copy to cover handling and mailing costs. (Prices and numbers are subject to change without notice.)

Name_____

Address_____

City_____ State_____ Zip Code_____
Allow at least 4 weeks for delivery

THE SILENT SIN:

A Case History of Incest

John Woodbury, Ph.D.,
and
Elroy Schwartz

A SIGNET BOOK from
NEW AMERICAN LIBRARY
TIMES MIRROR

COPYRIGHT © 1971 BY ELROY SCHWARTZ
AND JOHN WOODBURY, PH.D.

All rights reserved

SIGNET TRADEMARK REG. U.S. PAT. OFF. AND FOREIGN COUNTRIES
REGISTERED TRADEMARK—MARCA REGISTRADA
HECHO EN CHICAGO, U.S.A.

SIGNET, SIGNET CLASSICS, MENTOR, PLUME AND MERIDIAN BOOKS
are published by The New American Library, Inc.,
1301 Avenue of the Americas, New York, New York 10019

FIRST SIGNET PRINTING, AUGUST, 1971

5 6 7 8 9 10 11 12 13

PRINTED IN THE UNITED STATES OF AMERICA

PREFACE

During the first five of my twenty years in private practice as a clinical psychologist, I would occasionally find that incest was at the root of female patients' emotional problems. The pain it caused these women was intense, but its occurrence was relatively rare. During the past three or four years, however, I have noted a sharp increase in the number of cases, and I am amazed to discover that over 30 percent of the female patients in my current caseload has been subjected to an incestuous relationship.

In my graduate training at Washington State University I was taught that among the general population the incidence of incest was one per million. If these figures are accurate, it would appear that each case of incest that had occurred west of the Rockies had, in some manner, found its way into my office. Since this was obviously impossible, it was apparent that further investigation was necessary, particularly in view of the terrible psychological damage incest causes its victims.

In 1969, through the facilities of the California Mental Health and Child Guidance Service, I conducted an analytic and statistical survey of the incidence of incest in the clinical histories of female patients. Questionnaires were sent to 650 psychologists and psychiatrists in the United States, 483 (or 74.3 percent) of whom responded. On the basis of their replies, and taking into consideration such factors as the percent of the population who have been in psychotherapy, the percent who do not respond to psychotherapy, and the percent unlikely to admit such a relationship, the survey strongly indicates that the incidence of incest implicates at least 5 percent of the population and perhaps up to 15 percent. The probability is that if incest is not taking place in your own home—it is taking place on your street. In 1940, in a survey conducted by Riener, the incidence was shown to be one in a million; in 1950, in the survey conducted by Kinsey, it was one in one hundred. Today, it is one in twenty. That means that in the last thirty years there has been an astronomical increase of 50,000 percent in reported cases of incest.

—John Woodbury, Ph.D.

CONTENTS

Introduction	9
First Visit, November 1	18
Second Visit, November 7	23
Third Visit, November 14	43
A Telephone Call, November 17	67
Fourth Visit, November 18	69
Fifth Visit, November 19	94
An Interview with Paul, November 25	112
Sixth Visit, December 9	120
Seventh Visit, December 11	139
Eighth Visit, December 12	165
Ninth Visit, December 19	177
Tenth Visit, January 13	189
Eleventh Visit, January 24	198
Conclusion	209

INTRODUCTION

The word, "taboo" relates to a sacred prohibition against certain types of behavior that are considered unclean and dangerous to the species. Taboos are the oldest unwritten laws of primitive societies, predating the gods and even the hoariest of religions. Of all the taboos recorded in the annals of mankind, those against incest are the most universal, the most ancient, and the strongest. Some societies permit adultery, others premarital sex, but with few exceptions, incest has always evoked the strictest prohibitions.

In the beginning there were families only: a male and perhaps one, two, or three females and a number of children. As these families roamed the forests and the plains, they inevitably came into contact with other families. When this occurred, a battle would erupt to preserve the territorial rights of each family, and during the fighting members of the families would be severely injured, if not killed. It eventually occurred to the heads of these families that if they gave their daughters and/or sons for the purpose of a sexual union with members of another tribe, not only would the battles cease, but the families would form an alliance to protect their progeny. This revelation would not only stop them from warring against each other, but would provide strength for the two families to war against other families that functioned as a single unit.

Eventually the principle of strength through interfamilial union gained ascendance. Hence, evolved the practice of prohibiting a daughter from consummating a union with a member of her own family in order that she might be saved for union with a member of another family. This principle could be labeled a manifestation of cultural evolution, as contrasted to the biological type of evolution originally formulated by Darwin. In cultural evolution certain types of learned behavior increased the probability that a certain culture, and hence the people who practiced certain cultural behaviors, would survive.*

Another reason for the origin of incest taboos was the recognition by primitive societies that inbreeding produced adverse biological effects. Some of the deleterious effects thought to be found in offspring of incestuous relationships are albinism, certain forms of mental deficiency, deaf-mutism, dwarfism, and schizophrenia.

Also, incest taboos encourage marriage with other groups—which brings to the children of such unions additional genes that enhance the survival opportunities fittest in the biological sense. In addition, marriage between members of different groups promotes the dissemination of knowledge which, from a cultural standpoint, would also contribute to the survival of the fittest.

Whether or not there are even more reasons that we don't know about for the development of incest taboos, there is no question but that they have been lasting and they have been strong.

Interestingly enough, however, there was a time in history when incestuous relationships were prescribed to cure biological defects. For example, during the Middle Ages, incest was thought to help in the cure of syphilis and the black plague.

It is also a widely held belief that humans, by innate

---

*The principle also accounts for the ascendance of the Western cultures over other cultures when considered in light of so-called "developed" versus the "underdeveloped" nations.

"instinct," are naturally repelled by incest. This presents a rather paradoxical situation when viewed in relation to the Freudian theory of human behavior, which in essence would suggest that if a repugnance against incest were instinctive, it would not be necessary to formulate taboos against incest in the first place. Freud's theory implies that incest taboos are a reaction to incestuous wishes. They are a rejection of frightening childhood sexual attraction toward the parent of the opposite sex. As a consequence, the incestuous wishes are repressed into the unconscious and express themselves in disguised form through free-floating anxiety, belligerence, and sometimes neuroses and psychoses. Freud explains that such disturbances may arise when a thought is pushed into the unconscious. Then a peculiar phenomenon may occur. The idea associated with a particular thought or memory may be repressed, but the emotion continues to be active. As a consequence, we suffer the feelings of anxiety and/or frustration, but we are at a loss to explain why. These negative emotions may be transformed into physical or neurotic symptoms such as tension, headaches, ulcers, palpitations of the heart, obsessive thoughts, compulsive patterns of behavior, feelings of persecution, paralysis of the hand, functional deafness or blindness, and even death, as with the victims of a voodoo hex or the Korean prisoners of war who died from purely psychological causes called "give-up 'itis."

Keeping this in mind, we arrive at an explanation of much of the violence and chaos we are presently observing in our modern society—an explanation revolving around the concept of Oedipal conflict as originated by Freud in 1905 as follows:

One of Freud's earlier patients had described an incestuous relationship with her father that he later discovered to be a product of her fantasies. It was, however, an important discovery—so much so that in one of his later papers, Freud said, "If psychoanalysis could boast of no other achievement than the discovery of the repressed Oedipus complex, that alone would give it a claim to be included among the precious new acquisitions of mankind."

For Freud it really made little difference whether the incestuous act was real or fantasized. The fact remained that the desire for it was deeply and strongly imbedded in the unconscious. Freud's thesis was that during the early years of life a child competes with the parent of the same sex for the love of the parent of the opposite sex. In most instances, the child cannot, of course, defeat the parent with whom he is competing. Therefore, the normal resolution of the situation is for the child to identify with the parent of the same sex—to take on his personality characteristics and become as much like him as possible. There are times, however, when the problem is not resolved in this manner. A mother may despise her husband and substitute the son for the husband in her affections. In this instance the mother becomes the seductress of and the mistress to her son. In other instances the mother, because of a psychological aversion to sexual relations with the husband, may subtly encourage her daughter to assume the mother's role. The husband, if he is weak, may accept the shift. All of this may occur unconsciously, but when and if it does come to light, the mother will often blame the daughter.

In summary, Freudian theory would suggest that incestuous impulses are natural; that they have been repressed by extraneous social forces into the unconscious; that, although they are in the unconscious, they still exert psychological pressures; and that these pressures may manifest themselves in the form of a psychopathology called neurosis.

It follows that to cure the pathology, one releases the repressed material from the unconscious, which in turn removes the anxiety and guilt associated with the repressed idea. Unfortunately another type of pathology called the psychopathic personality may also be formed by psychological pressures. The difference between the psychopath and the neurotic (the latter being the type of personality with which Freud originally worked) is that the neurotic suffers from too strong a conscience while the psychopath suffers from too little. The neurotic has such a strong conscience that he is afraid of or would feel too guilty about openly expressing his aggressive or antisocial impulses. Therefore, he expresses his conflicts in a disguised or symbolic form, perhaps developing free-floating anxiety, ulcers, and other symptoms of his basic psychological problem. The psychopath, on the other hand, having no conscience, expresses his hostility and antisocial wishes openly. As a consequence, he is often the committer of crime and violence, which, of course, is the ultimate expression of hostility.

I have no doubts in my own mind that the Freudian theory, which was developed on the basis of analysis of a few neurotic patients living in a middle-class Jewish community in Vienna at the turn of the century, accounts for much of the uncontrolled social upheaval we are experiencing today. Freud's solution to psychoneuroses was to reduce the strength of the conscience—which works quite well with the psychoneurotic. But Freud had very little success in dealing with the psychopathic personality or the psychotic personality. His theory, however, was generalized to include all types of personalities, not just the neurotic. Thus, we will often find psychiatrists, psychologists, psychoanalysts, and other types of therapists advocating the reduction of guilt and responsibility in order to reduce the strength of the conscience even in individuals whose personality problems stem from the fact that their conscience is already excessively weak, thereby enabling them to act in an antisocial manner. Later on I will show the reader how certain therapists will blame everybody but the father in an incestuous incident.

How does incest begin? Weinberg states that a markedly abnormal and disorganized family situation was crucial for its onset.* In his study of 203 cases, he found that most of the participants were very immature, dependent, socially isolated people from a low socioeconomic background who were emotionally depriving, exploitative, and tolerant of promiscuity, adultery, and alcoholism. The parents were incapable of acting as adults. Interfamilial tension, conflict, and role confusion aggravated the already unstable family unit, which deteriorated even further upon discovery of the incestuous relationship.

It was particularly noteworthy that in father-daughter incest, the mother played a decisive role in the outcome of the problem. If the mother denied its existence, the incest continued for a long period of time. If she objected, the relationship quickly terminated. The father was almost always the aggressor and tended to initiate the relationship when his own abilities as a male were failing, when other females were becoming less accessible to him and when his daughters were maturing physically.

In a study by Bender, where pre-adolescent children were involved in incest, the girls were found to be attractive, frequently seductive attention-seekers who attempted to overcome feelings of emotional deprivation by genital contact with older males.† They did not appear to feel guilt.

In adolescent girls, however, stronger guilt reactions were elicited. This was ascribed to the increased strength of the conscience with the onset of puberty. Later, the subjects often compulsively sought, in a reckless, thinly disguised manner, to find a father substitute in their relationships with other males.

In other instances, it has been found that an intense rejection by the mother, combined with a passive type of father, were important in the girls' acceptance of the incestuous type of relationship as a way of life. These

*Weinberg, S. *"Incest Behavior."* New York: Citadel Press, Inc., 1955.
†Bender, L. *Dynamic Psychopathology of Childhood.* Springfield, Illinois: Charles C Thomas, Publisher, 1954.

A CASE HISTORY OF INCEST

girls also tended to look for father substitutes later in life.

How an incestuous relationship starts varies from case to case. Sometimes it develops out of what was initially, at least on a conscious level, an innocent expression of affection. The most common instance is where the daughter begins sleeping in bed with the father in the morning after the mother has arisen. This may be either at the father's invitation or through habit by the daughter, who became used to climbing in bed earlier in life when both the mother and the father were present. In cuddling the daughter, inadvertent contact in the genital area becomes pleasantly stimulating. This may be exacerbated by the fact that males frequently have an erection during the early morning hours due to the pressure of an extended bladder.

Sometimes a little girl is just curious and wants to explore. The father may allow her, due to a variety of reasons ranging from a desire to avoid causing her a "sexual trauma" by appearing to be repelled to the pleasure he feels from such a physical contact. If the husband is immature or if he has been rejected by his spouse, he may yield to temptation and increasingly encourage the activity until it develops into a consummated incestuous relationship.

The manifest symptoms of past incestuous experience in the grown woman are as numerous as the different types of deviant behavior. The most frequent are frigidity, nymphomania, and homosexuality, all of which may occur simultaneously in one person. Alcoholism is also common. In fact, I would strongly suspect that if one were to examine the etiology of alcoholic women in detail, one would find that an extraordinarily high percentage had been involved in incest at an early age.

Failure to achieve a climax is particularly prevalent following incest, and it was found that 93 percent of the hard-core lesbians in a local women's prison had been forced into incestuous relations at a very young age.

One inmate in the same institution hated the "male"

so intensely that in a rage she killed her only son, for no apparent reason, while not harming her three daughters. The reason became apparent, however, when in therapy, an earlier incestuous relationship proved to underlie her deep hatred. It is this hatred that is common in all cases of incest. It is hatred of the self, born out of the guilt felt for enjoying the relationship, and the hostility she experienced for having been debauched and defiled by those who should have loved her the most.

It should be obvious that the problems created by incest cannot be resolved by secrecy. However, prosecuting the offending male is a reaction that must be judiciously weighed. It may cause more harm than good. In the aforementioned study by Weinberg almost every psychiatrist interviewed ruled out informing the police about the crime. While I do not necessarily agree, there certainly are times when it would be exceedingly unwise. I feel the threat of prosecution is more effective, particularly when coupled with other conditions designed to rectify the psychic damage inflicted on the child and to insure that the crime is not repeated. Ordinarily, the best approach is to involve all of the significant members of the family in psychotherapy.

One of the most disturbing elements revealed in the present study is the tendency of some psychotherapists to place the entire blame for incest on the child and completely exonerate the adult. It may be true that the child may have behaved in a somewhat seductive fashion, but in all probability she was taught to do so. Not only is it normal for fathers to encourage their daughters to act in a very feminine way, but when a little girl has been introduced to sexual activities at a very early age by an adult, with no apparent objections from the mother, it seems only reasonable that she would develop an awareness of her sexual charms. Even if the child behaves seductively, can we really expect an eight- or nine-year-old girl to possess a greater sense of responsibility and self-discipline than say, a thirty-seven-year-old man? The attitude of removing the responsibility from the adult rewards the criminal and punishes the victim.

No person can truly appreciate all the problems and ramifications growing out of incestuous unions until he has fully explored a case history of one of its victims. The purpose of this book is to bring to you the actual feelings and thoughts of one of my patients as she relives, under hypnosis, her incestuous relationship with her father, and its effect on her later sexual experiences with other men.

Barbara's story provides a classic example of all the psychological problems that are the product of incestuous relations. If I were to quote a hundred more cases from my files, they would add no more to your knowledge and understanding than you will receive by reading the following history. If you find the content shocking and crude on occasion, it is because the experiences are recorded exactly as they happened and exactly as they were described. Only the names have been changed to protect the people involved.

First Visit,

NOVEMBER 1

The case history of Barbara began on October 30, 1968, when a friend called me, alarmed because a young girl he knew had been talking about taking her life. He explained that he was about to hire her to do some typing and did not know her very well. She'd told him her marriage was in the process of being annulled and she felt completely lost and alone. I agreed to see her and set a time for her to come in.

I had just finished with one appointment and was about to call my answering service to see if there were any messages, when I heard the outer door to my office open. I glanced down at the calendar and realized the next patient was the young lady my friend had called me about. I rose from my desk, crossed to the outer office, and looked in.

Barbara was seated just inside the doorway; she was dressed in a Navy pea jacket and mod bell-bottoms, yet looking prim, proper, a little apprehensive and quite subdued. A girl in her late teens, she was about five-feet-two or -three and weighed about one hundred and ten pounds. Her long blonde hair curved in bangs across her forehead, and dark lashes accentuated her almond-shaped eyes. She was attractive, although not beautiful. There was a glow to her face that characterized her from the first moment I saw her.

A CASE HISTORY OF INCEST 19

Thus began a strange association marked by an unexpected phone call, and a furtive visit that was to carry us both into her painful, surrealistic world.

Of course I did not know this as I introduced myself and asked her to come into my office. As she crossed the room to the door it was obvious that she was extremely self-conscious. She sat in the chair I indicated.

After some preliminary remarks, Barbara told me she didn't really know why she was here. She had come at the insistence of our mutual friend, a writer, whom she had met a relatively short time before. I asked her to tell me what was bothering her, and she told me that she had been having a great deal of difficulty with her marriage. She had married only recently, but her husband, Bob, seemed to have fallen out of love the moment they were married. Two weeks before, he had awakened her to say that he wanted her to leave the very next day. He hadn't given her any reason at that time, but subsequently said she had pushed him into the marriage, which she denied doing. She felt that he just couldn't accept the idea of being married.

They had been married six weeks, and until that point, Barbara felt that everything was "groovy" and hadn't realized there was any problem. I asked if there were any indications that her husband was unhappy.

She said, "Well, one thing. There have been a few problems in my past that have more or less affected my sex life, but after I started seeing a psychiatrist, Dr. Nillos, at my gynecologist's recommendation, they got better, at least I wasn't bothered by them anymore. But Bob couldn't accept that. He didn't feel they had."

"What grounds did Bob use for the annulment?"

"He said I hadn't told him about the problem I had before our marriage. But I *had* told him."

I asked, "What problem was that?"

And she replied, "I had some problems with incest with my father."

Intuitively, several questions immediately leaped to mind. Often many months, and sometimes years, of analysis are required before a patient will acknowledge an incestuous relationship. To express it so openly is highly unusual.

I was also impressed by the flatness of this girl's emotions as she revealed her difficulty. Most patients are so mortified with shame by their experiences that they stutter, stammer, and can only allude to them in the most evasive, circumstantial manner. But not Barbara. She imparted this information in a flat quiet monotone.

I wondered, Schizophrenic? Psychopath? Even her use of the word "incest" was unusual for a teen-age girl.

I hypothesized, "Intelligent. Previous psychotherapy."

These questions were temporarily stored away in another part of my mind to be pursued later. The time was not ripe to seek the answers now. It would be better to see first how she herself spontaneously regarded the problem without the intrusion of any questions from me.

These were the thoughts that flashed through my mind as I said, "Tell me about it."

She continued, still flatly, "It started at a very early age—at about five. And it went on until I was fourteen. But the problem doesn't exist now, only Bob won't believe me and he used this as grounds for annulment. He said I didn't tell him about it before our marriage, but I did."

I asked if she wanted to remain married to Bob, and she was most emphatic in saying she did.

I then asked her, "Do you think I can help you?"

She said, "I don't think so unless you can make me accept the fact that Bob is gone. I know my marriage is over and it's not easy to accept."

I knew she was not really asking me to help her accept the problem. I asked myself, What is she hiding?

I ignored her request and pursued a new tack in my quest for more information. I asked her to tell me more about what transpired between her and the psychiatrist Dr. Nillos. She said that she had told him the problem,

A CASE HISTORY OF INCEST

that Bob didn't really believe her—that he had never heard of such a thing as an incestuous relationship. But Dr. Nillos confirmed that what she was telling him was true. She had seen Dr. Nillos just once and then, although she had been recommended as the patient, her husband became the patient.

I asked her what Dr. Nillos had said during the first interview.

She replied, "He didn't tell me anything, except that incest was very normal—not normal, but a thing that happened. Often."

I asked if he had indicated that it might lead to problems, and Barbara said yes. I asked her if he had told her what these might be.

She said, "Dr. Nillos thought I had come through very well."

Barbara went on to tell me that she was seventeen years old, and had arrived in Los Angeles the preceding June from her home town. She had left home to avoid the constant demands of her father to continue their incestuous relations. She then related that she worked as a teller in a bank and that she paid her own doctor bills, clothes, carfare, and lunches. Her husband, a musician and not steadily employed, paid for the rent and their entertainment.

I probed the relationship with her father in an attempt to find out what her real emotions about it were. I asked, "How did you feel about your father's desire for you?"

She replied, "It didn't bother me. It doesn't bother me at all."

I asked if it had created any problems that she was aware of and she told me, "Just minor problems, but nothing now."

I asked if the psychiatrist had indicated that either she or Bob had a severe emotional problem.

She said, "No. No. He said I was crazy. I think he told Bob that."

Again my mind stored away an unstated observation —a tendency to deny a problem and then later confirm it by unconscious contradiction. I continued, "He told Bob that you were crazy?"

"I think so because Bob thought I should be committed to an insane asylum."

"Did he give any reason for this?"

"Yes. Because I was so messed up."

Barbara related that she had told Dr. Nillos about the "half-assed attempted suicide"—as she called it—when she was thirteen years old. It had happened while she was intoxicated after having been drinking with a group of choir children after rehearsal at church. The boy she was dating turned his attentions to another girl, and this upset Barbara so much that she ran to a nearby freeway, flung herself over a rail hoping a car would run over her. However, when no car approached for some minutes, she got up, brushed herself off, and walked to the nearest police station and asked them to call her parents, who came to pick her up.

She went on to relate that she believed the contributing factor in the breakup of her marriage was that her husband had very strong homosexual tendencies. He had been involved in homosexual relationships many times before their marriage and had lived with another couple. They had encouraged him to participate in a variety of sexual practices with both the man and his wife. I asked her if that had created any problem between them. She emphatically denied it, adding that his homosexuality had not even made him less desirable.

I questioned her further about any current thoughts of suicide. She denied that she had any real thought of acting upon them. I determined that this was true and brought our first meeting to an end. She did not consciously want help at this point and had only come to see me because of the insistence of our mutual friend. I said as much and at the same time I left the door open for her to return if she felt the need.

Second Visit,

NOVEMBER 7

Barbara called on November 4, and I arranged to see her on November 7 for our second visit.

When she arrived I noticed she was not wearing a coat, only a man's shirt tied beneath her breasts and hip-huggers that left her midriff bare. Her brown eyes were somber as she told me she had thought a great deal about our first meeting. She told me, too, that she had been quite upset during the week.

I asked her if she had been crying.

"Yes, every day, whether I need to or not."

"You've been crying every day?"

"Yes, every day when I go back to my room. It's so lonely, so lonely. Can you help me, Dr. Woodbury?"

I thought to myself, How can I honestly say I can help this girl? By this time I strongly expected she was a psychopath and would be extremely difficult to cure. Although she gave no evidence of it, I suspected that underneath the demure helplessness of the child existed the shrewdly manipulative machinations of a mature woman.

I decided the only chance for success lay in using a therapeutic technique with which I had been experimenting recently—one that I refer to as a "marathon hypnotic encounter." It involves placing subjects under an extremely deep, somnifacient state of hpynosis and having them relive, in minute detail, significant traumatic episodes of their past live's until they become intellectually exhausted and emotionally drained. These sessions often last up to four hours and are scheduled two to four times per week. Every word is recorded on tape and then transcribed into a written record.

Just before the patient is awakened from the trance at the end of each session, his memory of what has transpired during the session is blocked out. When the therapist determines that all the essential information has been extracted, the unconscious motivation revealed, and the inconsistencies resolved, the typewritten material is presented to the patient to read exactly as it was given. The patient may also listen to the original tapes if she so desires.

At this point, the conscious mind is forced to encounter the unconscious after both the conscious and unconscious defenses have been weakened by the exhaustive marathon hypnotic interrogation. Surprisingly, considerable improvement can be observed even before presenting the written material to the patient in a conscious state.

The reason this treatment is effective with a psychopath is that the patient is thus psychologically reborn. During this process, he or she acquires a set of values—the essential element most psychopaths lack.

I explained my treatment plan to Barbara. She was immediately apprehensive and extremely reluctant to agree to it. After ten minutes of explaining the program, Barbara acquiesed.

We moved to the special soundproof room I use for hypnotism and free association. I suppose I should call it my black room. There is a large black comfortable recliner for the patient and a large black executive swivel-chair for me. The patient faces a black velvet curtain behind which is a multicolor design that flashes in such away that different colors leap out and recede at the rate of six cycles per second—the same rate as the delta or sleep waves of the brain.

To the right is a black table. The room's walls are of

rich dark walnut and there is a muted red light overhead.

Barbara sat in the recliner and pushed it back. I dimmed the bright fluorescent lights and switched on the red one. Her face reflected the soft red glow. All else receded into the background.

I had no idea whether Barbara would be a good or poor subject. It can be difficult to place a psychopath under hypnosis. However, Barbara succumbed as quickly as any subject I have ever had. I turned on the tape recorder and what follows is a verbatim report of all the material that was obtained from the hypnotic sessions with Barbara except for those excerpts that were summarized to avoid redundancy.

I had no sooner reached the point of counting to three when Barbara's deep relaxed breathing quickly changed to short gasps and she began to twist uncomfortably in her chair.

I said, "You seem upset."

"I don't want to be hurt." Suddenly tears flowed from beneath her tightly closed lids.

"How do people hurt you?"

"Every time I do something for someone, then I find out I shouldn't have because they use it against me." Barbara began to sob lightly.

Through her sobs, she said, "I just don't want to be hurt. I don't want to be hurt anymore." The sobs became more pronounced and deeper.

I assured her I wasn't going to let this happen and asked who had hurt her the most.

"Bob. I've never loved anyone, ever, like him. I'd die for him. But he just leaves me out in the cold. He doesn't even care."

She seemed very tense now. Her hands were clasped in her lap, the knuckles white from the pressure she was exerting.

I continued to question her.

"The doctor said there was something wrong with you. You had to straighten something out."

Barbara, with her eyes closed and still in a state of

hypnosis, replied, "It wasn't that big a problem. Not to me."

"What is the problem?"

"With my dad. It wasn't that big a thing. I don't even care about it. It doesn't even bother me. It was a long time ago. It doesn't touch me now."

"Then it bothers Bob," I said.

"Yeah. I don't understand. He says I'm sick, and I'm not sick. I'm a little confused most of the time, but I'm not sick," Barbara replied.

"What are you confused about?" I queried further.

"Oh, little things, things that don't really make any difference. I mean, I don't understand some of my feelings. I don't understand how they began. I've been pretty shitty all of my life, and I've done a lot of things to hurt a lot of people, and did them deliberately. I don't understand how someone can love me. Just stuff like that. Things that don't really make any sense."

"Perhaps you hate yourself."

"No. I don't hate myself. I'm only disappointed in me, but I don't hate myself. I think I could be doing a lot better than I am."

"But you don't understand how people can love you," I said.

Barbara uncrossed her legs and shifted uncomfortably in her chair. She hesitated a moment and then said, "Oh, if you knew all the things I've done. All the horrid, horrid things I've done."

Barbara's defenses were now broken by her confession. She had let her guard down. I counted to five, putting her into an even deeper trance. Her body relaxed and her tears ceased. Therapy had begun.

"Can you tell me about the horrid things you've done? I think that's what's really bothering you."

Barbara was now answering without hesitation.

"I can tell you. It doesn't bother me to say it. Like using my parents—blackmailing my father to get what I wanted. I really did that. If he didn't do what I wanted, I wouldn't participate—I wouldn't let him do something. When he hurt me, I hurt him back. Just stuff like that."

"How would he hurt you?"

"He wouldn't let me do what I wanted. I'm awfully spoiled. I would—I'd just be real cold to him, or if he would make me mad in any way, I'd just strike back."

I knew that leading into the incestuous relationship with her father would uncover subconscious resistance at almost any level. I would have to probe gently and carefully and help her accept the things she would tell me under hypnosis.

"You were really very deeply involved with your father, weren't you?"

"Yes, very. I always said I would never marry. I even said that before I came down here to L. A.—before I got married. I would never marry anyone. I really thought I was in love with my own father."

"There are people who feel that way," I answered.

"But not that kind of love. Not the kind of love that would hurt so many other people. It's not good. It's wrong. I could never go back home. I know my father still feels the same. I know what would happen. It happened while I was up there three weeks ago. I just can't take it anymore. I just don't believe in it. I don't love him anymore—not like I did. And it hurts him because I don't—and I don't want to hurt him. He didn't mean to do it."

I couldn't believe she didn't love him "like I did" nor, as a matter of fact, did I believe she didn't want to hurt him. Although her conscious resistances relaxed with her confession, I was now encountering other resistances stemming from what Jung would call the "collective unconscious," plus the instinctual reaction against incest that began in the very womb of man's existence and developed over hundreds of generations of mother-daughter confrontations.

"Barbara, your relationship with your father bothers you a lot more than you realize."

"No, it doesn't bother me. It really doesn't. It doesn't hurt me ever, but it's hurt them. One time I even told my mother that I used my father to get what I wanted. I told her I'd use him to the end of my life to get anything I wanted. I told her that. It was so cruel. So unfair. I hurt them both so much."

"You were angry with your mother."

"No! No, not with my mom—with my dad. I was furious with him."

"But you said you were cruel to your mother."

"I was cruel to her."

"Then you must have been angry with her to be cruel."

"I was angry with her because she wouldn't divorce him. But if she had, I'd have hated her for it."

"You wanted her to divorce your father? Why was that?"

"Because I wanted to get away from him. So he'd have to leave me alone. I wanted to be with my mother. My mother and I were never close, and I loved her so much, but she would never do anything with me. She wouldn't go to the Brownies with me, she wouldn't do anything. She rides motorcycles. She never dresses up and she never wears makeup. She doesn't even hardly comb her hair. I just wish she'd have been a real mother and been around when I needed her, but she was never there. Never."

"Your mother was never a real mother; she was never there when you needed her, but you didn't hate her?"

"No. I don't hate her. It was only natural for her to be jealous of me because of my father. I commanded all of his attention. If my father had never started, then mom and I would have been close. I was her first daughter."

At this point, I decided to regress the patient in time, regress her to the original incestual relationship.

I told her, "Barbara, I'm going to put you into a much deeper sleep, a much deeper sleep. We are going back to the very beginning. One. I want you to go into a deeper sleep. A deeper sleep. A deeper sleep. You will be in a deep sleep by the time I reach three. Sleep very sound, sleep very deep. Two. Deeper and deeper asleep. Three. A very sound, a very deep sleep, Barbara. The relationship with your father—how did it all start? Can you remember the first time,"

There was a pause. Barbara stirred and mumbled something I didn't understand. I asked her to repeat it slowly and more distinctly.

She said, "In a Quonset hut in Corpus Christi."

"How old were you?"

"I'm three."

There was a long pause. I waited for Barbara to say something more, and when she didn't, I said, "You were three years old. How do you feel now?"

Barbara giggled and said, "My head feels so big."

I unconsciously reacted to her statement and said unthinkingly, "Your head feels big, yes. That's because you are three years old. You head will feel big, because it's bigger than your body when you're three."*

Barbara laughed.

I continued, "Didn't you know that?" I waited until Barbara had stopped laughing and then tried to reset the scene she had begun. "Your father is playing with you," I began.

"Let's talk about something else. I can't get it out of my head."

"Relax, Barbara, you can't get it out of your head. You want to get it out of your head though, don't you?"

"Yes. Yes. Yes," Barbara mumbled.

I continued, "The only way you can get it out of your head is to tell me. That will get it out of your head. Barbara, listen to me before we start talking. I understand how you feel. I understand that part of you is unhappy about it, but part of you was very happy about it. Part of you cried, and part of you enjoyed it."

Barbara shook her head violently and said, "That's bad!"

---

* I knew the concept was correct, i.e., her head being so much bigger than her body, but something was wrong. I wasn't to learn for many months what that was.

I answered, "Why do you say that's bad?"

Barbara shook her head again and moaned, "I was so young. . . ."

"That's right. You were so young. Can you remember what you were wearing?"

"I remember like a picture," Barbara said. She stirred uneasily in her chair. Her hands clasped each other tighter. She changed the position of her legs and then went on, "I was wearing a white dress, kind of like a fluffy white. I had just gotten out of the hospital—I think it was the hospital. My dad told me I was in the hospital. I had some kind of disease. I was so sick I almost died. My mother didn't want to look at me. I didn't have any teeth."

"What happened to your teeth?"

"I never grew any, I was so sick. I didn't even have any hair." Barbara laughed and continued, "I was funny-looking."

"You thought you were funny-looking, or did you feel like you were ugly?"

Barbara answered, "I was funny-looking. I was tall and skinny and I didn't have any teeth or hair. But my daddy still loved me. He still loved me."

The patient went on to say that she never felt that her mother loved her. She corrected that to say it wasn't that she didn't love her, but she felt she never liked her. Her mother never wanted her or any of the children around.

It was becoming quite obvious that the patient was trying to steer the conversation away, even while under hypnosis, from talking about the relationship with her father. I decided that was the relationship from which to begin analysis and I pressed my point further.

I said, "The relationship with your father started when you were three. Tell me about it."

Barbara stirred uneasily. She tried to break herself out of her hypnotic sleep and I had to relax her and count her back into a deep somnambulistic state. Then I repeated my request.

"I don't want to talk about it. My mommy and daddy

A CASE HISTORY OF INCEST 31

always told me I wasn't to talk about things like that. Those words were naughty."

I was determined not to let the patient digress another time. I said to her, "And your daddy did this with you when you were only three?"

"Yes, but he told me not to tell anyone, so I won't tell anyone."

"How did you feel when he told you not to tell your mother?"

"We had a secret. I never had a secret before."

"That was your first secret."

"After that I couldn't keep secrets at all."

"You never told anyone at all?"

"Daddy told me not to."

Before I could say anything, Barbara continued, "I wish I'd told."

"Who do you wish you'd told?"

"My mommy."

Under further questioning, I learned from Barbara that when she was quite young—she really wasn't sure what her age was—she remembered sitting underneath a table while her parents argued and yelled at each other. It impressed her because she had never heard them yell at each other before. She remembered crying. Yet, no matter how deeply I regressed her and tried to get her to remember or recall the words that her parents used at that particular moment, she could not. All she could remember was that her dad had told her mom something that she wouldn't believe. That it was about her father and her, Barbara. He wanted help from his wife, but she wouldn't believe him. She just couldn't bring herself to accept what he was saying.

Once again I tried to bring us back on the track. I said, "You said the first time your daddy did this with you was in a Quonset hut."

"Yes. That's where Navy people live."

"Where was your mother when you did this?"

"Most of the time it was at night and she was in bed. You can't wake my momma up when she's sleeping. My daddy used to take us to the bathroom at night before he would go to bed."

"I see. Then what would happen?"

I waited for Barbara to answer, but she began to shake her head violently. I pursued the matter. "He'd take you to the bathroom—don't wake up now, just relax, that's it—relax. Okay . . . your mommy was asleep. . . ."

Barbara began to cry, to sob almost hysterically. While she cried, I realized she was reliving a traumatic experience. Yet she had been so open and frank about the problem of incest with her father that I wondered what the crying and violent shaking of her head indicated. For some reason she couldn't bring herself to unlock the memories. What was the deep pain they were causing? Actually, at that moment, I wasn't sure whether I wanted to unlock those memories or not. Such a release could propel her into a deep psychosis. I decided to pursue her resistance and asked why she was crying.

Then Barbara gave me a way to unlock the memories.

She said, "I don't want to talk about it. I don't want to be *me* anymore."

She had given me the key! Create an alter ego!

I asked, "Who would you like to be?"

"Somebody who never has bad things happen."

"All right. Let's talk about somebody else then."

"Okay."

"Let's talk about a new person for a while. What shall we call her?"

"Ummmm . . . I don't know."

"Tell me her name."

"Ah, how about . . . how about Cindy?"

"Cindy. Fine. And where does Cindy live?"

"In a Quonset hut."

I must admit, I felt elated and excited. Her response was a classic example of the unconscious mind finding a way to circumvent the horror it had known in the past—a horror the conscious mind could not face. As sometimes happens, the unconscious mind provided the answer—she could only view her relationship with her father through the eyes of a third person, Cindy. I relaxed for a moment, knowing that the next part of the questioning would bring answers from the very depths of Barbara's mind. I wasn't to learn until much, much later the extent of the depths.

I said, "All right, Cindy lives in a Quonset hut and she has a secret. Let's talk about Cindy. I want you to tell me about Cindy. Cindy is a beautiful girl—a lovely girl. Once she went to the hospital. She was very, very sick. She came home. Then what happened?"

"Cindy's mommy and daddy took her to the hospital every day and then they put her in the hospital and all the doctors came and they all looked at her. But nobody knew what was wrong—nobody knew what was wrong. She couldn't eat anything at all. Everytime she'd eat, she'd get sick, so they had to put needles in her arms. They even fed her with needles in her arms. And she was really, really sick. And she didn't have any hair or any teeth. She was ugly, ugly, ugly. Someday she'd be pretty though, someday. But she came home, and her mommy didn't like her anymore because she said Cindy was too much trouble, and she didn't want her anyhow. But her daddy loved Cindy, and her daddy was always nice to her and brought her presents and stuff, because he didn't want her to die. And she lived, and he was happy. And then one night he took her to the bathroom and gave her a bath 'cause mommy was gone."

"How did Cindy like that?"

"She didn't like that because she was a tomboy. And her brothers—her little brother was littler than her and she could beat him up. But her daddy gave her a bath, and you know, you have to wash real good."

"Uh-huh, that's right."

"So, her daddy was washing her. But, he washed her really too good. Then she got dried off and she had to go to bed. And her daddy came in to take her to the bathroom before he went to sleep. And he acted like he was washing her again. Only with his hand."

"What did he wash her with the first time?"

"A washrag."

"And she had to go to the bathroom, and he started washing her again with his hand, only he really wasn't washing her."

"He was just pretending. Cindy didn't understand."

"That's right. She didn't understand, did she? Did Cindy feel bad about it, or did she just not understand?"

"She just didn't understand. She didn't even think about it."

"Did her daddy seem excited when he pretended to wash her?"

Barbara started to cry almost immediately. She cried deeply and emotionally. I counted to three, counting her back into a relaxed sleep. After her crying had subsided, I restated the question, "Did her daddy seem excited when he pretended to wash her?"

Barbara hesitated, and then softly said, "Yes."

"That upsets you. Why does that upset you?"

"Because Cindy was really a nice little girl."

A most interesting phenomenon had begun to develop. Barbara had begun to slip back and forth into her identity as Cindy and as herself in her unconscious. When the thoughts became too abhorrent to her conscious mind, she became Cindy. When they were not, she referred to herself as herself. In response to my question, "Why does that upset *you?*" Barbara answered, "Because *Cindy* was really a nice little girl."

"She's still a nice little girl. Do you know that?" I reassured her unconscious.

"If that thing had never happened, Cindy would be a nicer girl. She wouldn't have had so many problems."

"That's true. If that hadn't happened, Cindy wouldn't have had problems, but she's still a nice girl."

But Cindy's unconscious guilt, even as a three-year-old child, could not be pacified.

A CASE HISTORY OF INCEST 35

She said, "Cindy used to try to do things like that with all the little boys."

"Yes, her daddy taught her that," I again reassured her.

"But that's no good. That's no good at all."

Since the patient was in such a deep somnambulistic state, I again made a concerted effort to relieve the terrible guilt she had suffered ever since she was a child.

I told her, "It wasn't good for Cindy because it upset her, but that didn't make Cindy a bad girl. She couldn't help it. Cindy was a very nice girl and she always will be. She may have some problems, but she was always a nice girl—even when her hair and teeth were gone."

"Oh, she was so ugly. God, she was ugly," Barbara said, and then laughed and seemed to relax.

Her guilt appeared to have lessened so I again tested her feelings about her relationship to her father. "Okay, so her daddy taught Cindy to like that, didn't he? Because her daddy was sick, right?"

"Yes, and Cindy didn't know that he was sick. Not then. Not then."

"You wouldn't expect a three-year-old girl to know that, would you?"

"No. Her daddy was nice to her, but her mommy was never nice to her. Her mommy never had time for her. Cindy used to try to be with her mommy. She used to try to help her mommy iron and do like mommy would tell her to do. But her mommy would always tell her to go away."

"Cindy tried desperately to get her mommy to love her, didn't she? But mommy always made her feel as though something were wrong."

"She was so ugly. There was no reason why mommy should have loved her. She was so ugly."

It was obvious that a pattern had already established itself in Barbara's life that would be with her forever unless ameliorated. The concomitant feelings about the incest and ugliness instilled a deep sense of inferiority—a feeling of unworthiness. She then related how Cindy could not get along with anybody, that she had no friends, but her ambivalence was revealed by her statement that Cindy avoided friendships because she felt others could never accept her as she was. She attributed it to her ugliness. In reality her feelings were a projection of her guilt about her father. She attempted to deny her femininity by assuming the identity of a boy. She even developed a pride in this. She said she could fight with the best of them; she was the best cowboy, and when she had a boat, she could catch more crabs and cook them better than any of the boys.

Interestingly enough, she often confused guy and girl in her narration—a slip that manifested her unconscious desire to be a boy. I questioned her further about the conflict she felt about her feminine role and she stated that the guy-girl feeling was a nice one because she felt she could do better than either a boy or a girl. She explained further that "Cindy's mommy had to go to work when they came back from Formosa, and Cindy had to be the mommy. She had to learn to cook and she had to learn to be the mommy. It wasn't easy, but Cindy did it because everybody said she had to do it. Her mommy was always tired when she came home from work, and she'd go right to bed because she was so tired. So Cindy had to clean the house. And Cindy used to get so mad at her little sister because she didn't have to do anything."

Her derivation of the word Cindy dawned upon me, and I said, "Cindy is Cinderella."

"Only this Cindy never grew up to be pretty. She never had a fairy godmother, never had a pumpkin, never had mice, birds, or flowers, or a beautiful dress. She never had a Prince Charming. She had one, but he was a bum."

"How is that?"

"Because her Prince Charming was a shit-ass. He stopped caring just like that, because he decided he shouldn't. That's not a Prince Charming."

"Not much of one, anyway."

"That's a bum."

"It must be very painful to love a bum."

"It is because you can't stop loving him, even though he is. And you want to—you want to hate him, but you can't even do that. You couldn't hurt him if you had to."

"That's what makes Cindy a real woman, doesn't it?"

"It makes Cindy a stupid shit. If she had an ounce of brains, she'd go out and get herself knocked up and have a baby. Then she'd have something. She'd have something to hold on to, something to care about. Something to love, something to love her back."

"Cindy would only love her child, and the child would only love Cindy?"

"If Cindy could ever find a man who was a real man, Cindy could love a man too."

I decided to let Barbara relax and sleep while I looked back at the notes I'd been making during our hypnotic discussion. I counted her into a deeper sleep and then told her to relax, to breathe deep and to sleep very deeply. I searched the notes, trying to assimilate the material she'd given me up to this point. I searched for discrepancies between her conscious and unconscious mind that might reflect a deeper meaning. The hostility toward both her mother and father was quite obvious from the outset. This, of course, was in complete contradiction to her conscious mind. She was able to express some hostility toward her mother on an unconscious level, as evidenced by her remark, "She was never a real mother," but unable to express it on a more conscious level. Barbara would not openly express any anger or hostility toward her father, consciously or unconsciously. She remembered him as having always loved her, peculiarly perhaps, but always loving her.

Her hostility was masked by guilt and feelings of inferiority. Her guilt stemmed from the fact that she innately sensed that incest was wrong, but she enjoyed it. Not only did she enjoy it, but she introduced sexual experiences to other children. This added to the guilt she already felt. It is this heightened sense of guilt plus the excruciating excitement of sexual stimulation that irrevocably causes certain types of sicknesses in our children—such as nymphomania, homosexuality, drug addiction, alcoholism, fetishism, voyeurism, exhibitionism, and many other afflictions.*

Barbara attempted to relieve her guilt by contaminating others. I investigated this by stating, "You were telling me Cindy used to play with the boys like daddy."

"Yes. Under a box. A wooden crate."

"How did that start?"

"It was a game of hide-and-seek. You go in and take off all your clothes and everybody grabs one thing and throws it out. Then you find your clothes and put them on."

"How old was Cindy when she played that game?"

"She was in the first, second, third, and fourth grades."

"She played it a long time."

"And it progressed."

"How did it progress?"

"Well, then you not only took off all your clothes, but you tried out what you had. It was a terrible game."

Here, concisely stated, was Barbara's attitude toward sex. "Why do you say 'terrible'?"

"Because—it was sinful. It was dirty. It was nasty."

"How could it be nasty?" I probed.

"It wasn't right."

"I don't understand. How was it nasty?"

"Boys and girls just don't do things like that."

"But boys and girls do. Think about that. Boys and girls do."

"Cindy's not supposed to. If her daddy would ever find out, he'd probably break her neck."

Daddy would break her neck out of jealousy, not because he felt it was wrong. Cindy, however, did not

* An excellent example of this guilt plus excitement making for a hopelessly habit-forming situation is to be found in Vladimir Nabokov's novel, *Lolita*. One wonders whether the author realized he was accurately describing the common psychological effects of an incestuous relationship.

know this. I hesitated, but then asked, "But it was all right if her daddy did it?"

"Her daddy loved her."

She went on to relate that the game under the box never progressed much beyond the disrobing. They did engage in some "touch" play but that was the extent of it, partly because the ground was too wet. She played the game in Formosa with the children of other officers. The game came to an abrupt end when the boys' mothers found out about it. In talking about her relationship with these boys a tremendous competitive spirit between her and the boys became evident. I explored this facet further by asking her if the boys were treated differently than girls or if they looked different than girls.

She smiled, "They look kind of—they weren't made the same."

"How was that?"

"You know."

"I don't know from Cindy's standpoint. How would she have felt about it?"

"They looked funny. They didn't look right. They weren't made like I was made."

Again Barbara slid from Cindy to herself: "They weren't made like I was made." This was an indication that treatment was progressing for she exhibited less of a need to disguise her conflict. I tested her ability to face herself by asking her directly how she felt about herself, pointing out that the boys had something she didn't.

"I thought that I—that they had too much."

"I see."

"That I had what was right and they had too much."

"How did your daddy feel about your boyfriends?"

"He didn't like them. I couldn't understand why he didn't like them. They were all really nice boys. But he never really thought about them as being boyfriends or anything, because that's when I was a tomboy. We used to jump off a shed, and it was about twenty feet high.

And we'd have to grab ahold of a swing on the way down, and I was the only one who would do it, at first. The swing was only about five feet off the ground, and if you'd miss it—you'd had it. I never got scared. I used to do stuff like that. And we had a three-story tree house in an oak tree that was a hundred years old. And I pushed my little sister out of it, and she broke her wrist and got a concussion."

"How did you feel about that?"

"Terrible. I wanted to die."

"Why did you push her off?"

"We were having a water fight. She was on the other side and she wanted to be on our side, and I didn't really want her to. We never got along too well. But I let her be on our side, and I told her not to get on the third story because it's awfully high—taller than any house around. It was a big, big oak tree. The top was three stories high. I told her not to come up there anyhow. I got mad at her and pushed her, and she fell off."

"You were angry with your sister."

"I was always angry with her. I tried to kill her."

"How old were you when you tried to kill her?"

"I was eight. Instead of hitting her I always tried to strangle her, and I had my hands around her throat, and her face got white and she passed out."

"What stopped you?"

"Because she turned white. She passed out—you don't keep going. I was mad at something stupid. And I have never hurt anybody like that since. I could never hurt anyone again."

I have a private, unlisted number that is never used by anybody except my answering service in case of an emergency. It rang at this particular moment. I quickly counted Barbara into a deep sleep and let her relax while I took the call. When the call was over I turned back toward Barbara and saw that her whole body was shaking and her head twisting and turning violently. I said, "Barbara, you just remembered something. What was it?"

It was some moments before Barbara answered. Her breath came in short gasps. I repeated the question. Then Barbara said, "One time I saw my daddy and my mommy in bed at night."

"How did you feel about that"

"I didn't like it. They were so close. I wanted to talk to my daddy. He didn't even come in to talk to me. Even though he was there."

"He wouldn't come in and talk to you?"

"No. They didn't hear me when I knocked on the door, so I just opened it to see if they were asleep. But they weren't."

"Did it look like your daddy was hurting your mommy?"

"No. She was happy."

"How were they lying?"

"I don't remember."

"You do remember, and it does bother you. But you have to get it out, and then you'll feel better."

"I didn't think my daddy particularly liked my mommy."

"You didn't think your daddy liked your mommy?"

"No, but he did. He really did. I didn't like it."

"You didn't like it when they were happy with one another."

"They shouldn't have been doing that."

"Shouldn't have been doing what?"

"I don't know what they were doing. My daddy did that with me though. He liked me."

"Ah. This was a sign of love when he did it with you."

"Yeah. And he did it with my mother too."

"How did you feel about it when he did it with your mommy?"

"I don't understand why he did it, being as he was always yelling at mommy. He didn't yell at me."

"How did you feel when you saw him doing this to her? Did it make you angry or sad or afraid or happy?"

"It scared me."

"It made you afraid."

"Then I went back to my bedroom and I went to bed, but I couldn't sleep. I don't want to talk about it."

Barbara's jealousy of her mother was obvious, but her jealousy was completely unacceptable, even to her unconscious mind. I left this subject temporarily and returned to an old area of contention to probe deeper in an effort to extend her ability to tolerate the pain of her guilt.

I forgot my strategy for a moment and said, "Now Barbara, your daddy started out by washing you, and I guess he continued for a while just pretending he was washing you. And then he probably began doing other things, too. Can you tell me about that?"

"No."

"Can Cindy tell me?"

"Cindy told me not to tell you."

I had to smile at Barbara's response. I said, "Cindy's pretty smart, too, isn't she?"

I told Barbara I was going to let her go into a deeper sleep and then I was going to awaken her, and I emphasized that she would not remember anything we had talked about while she was under hypnosis. I explained that I would let her remember, at the proper time, but now now. I emphasized this again and again before I awakened her.

And that was the end of the second visit with Barbara.

Third Visit,

NOVEMBER 14

When Barbara came in, I asked her if she'd been crying as much as the last time. She told me she was crying as often but not as intensely. I asked if anything was new. She mentioned that the night before a boy she knew asked her to drop some acid with him. She told him no, but perhaps later in the week. She then suggested that I should talk to her while she was on a trip. I asked if she had dropped acid before and she told me she had, lots of times. I asked her how much, and she replied from 500 to 1000 micromilligrams on several occasions. The thought of brain damage crossed my mind.

"Isn't that kind of heavy?"

"I don't seem to be able to get off with less than 500. I think you could learn a lot more about me if I were on a trip."

I countered, "Tell you what, Barbara, I would really prefer you didn't drop any more acid. If you like, though, I could let you go back and relive some of your trips through hypnosis."

Barbara acted surprised. She giggled. And then she asked, "Could you really?"

"Uh-huh."

"That'd be groovy. That's out of sight."

"All right, then relax, Barbara. Relax in your chair.

Make yourself comfortable—I'm going to count to ten. As I count, your eyelids will grow heavy and you'll fall into a sound, deep sleep. Relax, Barbara. Relax and sleep."

Barbara was becoming more attuned to my voice and she quickly went into a sound, deep sleep. After the ten count, I counted to five to place her into a deeper sleep. I tested her for her state of hypnosis and found, once again, that she was in a deep somnifacient trance.

I must admit I had certain reservations about what was going to happen. Although I had used hypnosis a great deal in my work, and I have regressed patients under hypnosis, I had never before regressed a patient into an LSD trip. Those of my patients who had been on trips, through the use of various drugs, had described them to me from time to time. But to have a patient relive a trip in a state of regression under hypnosis was something new. I couldn't help but feel that a hypnotic trip would be better than the real thing.

I started off by saying, "Barbara, I want you to recall a good trip; a nice trip where the colors are pretty; where the colors were very, very beautiful and you felt you knew everything that was important. You felt you had the key; you had the knowledge. Tell me about that trip. What was it like?"

"I've been on a lot of good trips."

"Tell me about the first one, was it a good trip?"

"Yes, but I didn't get off too good. I didn't get loaded too good because I was afraid."

"The type of trip I want you to take, Barbara, is one where you're not afraid. Where you're not afraid to talk about everything."

"All right."

"What was the trip like, Barbara?"

"I was working for Kandor Machine Enterprises before I took the acid. And I really liked the job, but I had to say the words 'Kandor Machine Enterprises' so often. And in my trip, I was like a book. If you looked at me, you could read across my face and words were written down my body like a book. Except I would be looking through the back of the page, you know? And they were all written in beads. I love beads. And it would say in big, big letters. 'Kandor Machine Enterprises' in beads. And it was just like, you know, like the big lights on the movie theaters. And then, I saw all my troubles. They were all like pens, written—long shafts. The words were written in beads and all the troubles I had were tied in like shafts of wheat, and then, I was really worried about them because I couldn't understand why they were tied like that. I think that's when I got afraid of fire. It was after this trip, but it was—it's not a bad fear. And all of a sudden the wheat burned up along with all my troubles. Completely burned. They just—in a flash of fire.* Everything that hung me up was written in beads, on big shafts and they burned. All of them burned up. And then I saw tools made out of beads. Like hoes and rakes and stuff. They were all made out of beads—fluorescent colored beads. And when I was having the trip, I was laying next to a guy in a bathtub. It was very dark, except for two candles. And then the candles seemed to grow brighter and brighter and colors seemed to flash all over the place. I was telling him about my trip, and he was really getting off good, and he hadn't taken any acid at all. Afterwards we used to joke about it because he'd ask me if I'd seen any green hoes lately—this is mainly what I saw, and I was telling him about it. They were bright chartreuse green. This trip lasted about seventy-two hours because I had taken STP. In the trip everything was colors—beautiful, beautiful colors. And I saw like chicken wire and half of it was Paisley print and half of it was a Scotch plaid. Just beautiful things. I couldn't believe how beautiful everything was, and I felt like I could tell you anything. Anything that happened I could tell you. In the past. In the future. It didn't matter—I could tell you about it. And I could tell you the feelings of the people involved. I could see people and I could see their minds like I could read them. I

* The image of fire occurs again and again. Its meaning becomes clear later.

could look at them and tell you what they were thinking. And they were all grooving. They were grooving because Bob Dylan was on the radio, and he's really an out-of-sight guy.

"Then we were looking at albums and the albums changed colors and everything was really flashing. They had posters on the walls, and, oh, everything was so groovy I couldn't believe how groovy everything was. There were beads and there were bells, and they were all ringing. Oh, it was the grooviest trip; I can't believe how it was. And the next night everybody got busted. And I was there, and I got busted, too. But I got off because I didn't really have anything to do with it and I was going to testify for Buddy. Then I didn't testify because Buddy got caught again, and this time it was for good. He got put away. But that trip was so groovy, and I was so spaced; and when they were busting us, I was so loaded. And the cops were so funny because they'd try to talk to me and I couldn't talk to them. They asked for my I.D., and I said, 'Groovy, take it.' And then they'd say, 'Can we look through your purse?' And I said, 'I don't care if you look through my purse.' And they said, 'Well, do you want to watch?' And I said, 'No, I don't want to watch. I trust you, you're a cop.' And they said, 'You'd better watch, young lady.' So I watched and they looked through my purse. Everybody told me they were going to stash some grass on me if I didn't watch—so I watched. And I really didn't think they'd do anything, and they didn't. But they put me under surveillance. And, it was so funny, especially because I was stoned, because it stood out like a sore thumb. I couldn't believe it."

While Barbara had been describing her trip to me, I contemplated combining her hypnotic LSD trip with free association to probe even further into her locked secrets. Although I had stated earlier that her frank revelation of incest with her father was quite unusual, only a thin veneer of her unconscious mind had been tapped. The unconscious can best be described as a huge bank vault. Within the vault, there are many safety

A CASE HISTORY OF INCEST 47

deposit boxes, each one of them locked. You can get into the vault, but the significant contents are hidden inside the innumerable safety deposit boxes. Barbara's admission of incest was like opening the vault. But the key to her cure lay in the secret feelings embedded deep within the tightly guarded recesses of her mind. The prerequisite of a cure was the full understanding of these guilt-ridden contents.

We had unraveled some secrets, but many more remained to be revealed. As Barbara was such an excellent hypnotic subject, I decided to combine the regression into a trip with free association to probe even deeper.

"Barbara, I'm going to count to five. When I reach five, you'll feel like you just dropped acid. You'll be on a trip. You'll open your eyes and you'll see beautiful colors. One. You're on the trip. It's beautiful, beautiful. A beautiful trip. Two. Your mind is beginning to feel like it's on the trip. You'll be able to see the colors. Three. You're going deeper and deeper in the trip. Deeper and deeper in the trip. Four. You're going deeper and deeper and deeper. You feel good. Your mind is free. Your mind is relaxed. You're going to be able to answer any question that I ask while you're on the trip. You're going to be free. Very, very, free. I will interrupt you occasionally to ask you questions. Five. I want you to open your eyes. You're still hypnotized, Barbara, but open your eyes."

Barbara slowly opened her eyes. She gazed around the room, a half smile on her face. She grabbed for my hand and said, "Are you with me?"

"I'm with you. You have nothing to be afraid of. It's very, very beautiful. It goes all through your mind. It goes all through your body. It makes you very, very warm. Very, very secure. You feel good."

"I'm not hurting. It's groovy. It's out of sight."

"Barbara, you're going to go back, back, back in your mind. You feel good. Your life is an open book now. No secrets. It's very, very open. You're really going to live it, and that's what makes life so nice.

You're going to live it, and you're going to feel good about it. You're going to feel happy about it. You're going to feel happy to share it. You're going back deeper and deeper. Back, back. Now your eyes are heavy. Your eyes are very, very heavy. They're closing, closing, closing. You're going into a deep, deep sleep. A very deep sleep. You're going to tell me how it was with your father. What affected you the most?"

Barbara reiterated that the events began when she was three years old. He had bathed her and then later that night, when he took her to the toilet, he'd begun to "massage her" again. She described the feeling as being a very strange sensation. She said that it was pleasant and that it tickled. She remembered telling her father, "Daddy, that tickles." No matter how much I probed, she wasn't sure if the massaging took place over a two-day, two-week, or two-month period of time. She had no way of knowing, no way of remembering how long these events went on. I then asked her, "When did this pattern of massaging you change?"

She said, "One day he kissed me on the stomach, and then he kissed me—he kissed me there. From then on, that was basically the whole idea. It seemed strange to me. We always talked before. We'd talk about anything and everything that I would want to talk about."

"Now, your father began kissing you on the stomach and then he started kissing you on the vagina. Were you aware of the difference?"

"Yes. It was much different. It was warm. I didn't understand why he was doing it. He said, 'Because I love you. This is showing you that I love you.'"

"Try to describe your feelings. The feelings and thoughts that went through your mind."

"It tickled, yet I realized it was affection. That's the only real feeling I remember. It was the same thing even when I was older. I didn't understand it, so it didn't mean anything more than a tickle. But it hurt when he tried to put his finger in."

"It hurt?"

"Yes. I was very small. I was a very, very small girl. I was eight or nine before he could, I think."

"Did he try, at that time, to insert anything else?"

"His tongue. One time I remember he tried to kiss me on the mouth and I wouldn't let him. I'd never let him do that."

"Why?"

"It sounds dumb, but holding hands or just a quick kiss on the lips means more to me than anything. It has more feeling to it. It's dumb. I guess because I was involved in sex itself so long, it lost its meaning."

"You wouldn't let him kiss you on the mouth."

"I couldn't stand it. I just couldn't. I never have been able to."

"From anybody or just your father?"

"Just my father. And I won't let just anybody kiss me. It means too much."

"Kissing seems to hold particular significance for you."

"My father kissed me other places."

"He kissed you other places besides the vagina?"

"Yes, but not for a long time. I started wearing a bra when I was in the fourth grade, and then he would kiss me on the breasts. This always repulsed me. I couldn't stand it. It seemed—I don't know, maybe because I was used to the other. I don't know. But I hated it because it tickled, and I can't stand to be tickled. That was all I could relate to it. Now I realize it was much more involved, but at the time, that was all I could think of."

"What do you realize is involved now?"

"Sexual stimulation. A turning on. But at the time, it didn't turn me on. It was nothing more than an affectionate game as far as I was concerned. But when I started growing up—when I started into high school, I guess, was the first time I realized what it was, and all these years my father had said, 'You save yourself for your husband.' And yet, here he was—taking me. It didn't add up. It didn't make sense."

"How did you feel about it?"

"I guess I sort of hated him, but really a false hate because I couldn't really hate him. I don't think you can really hate anyone that loves you. As soon as I realized what was involved, I wanted it to end. I wanted it to end because I wanted to be a virgin for my husband. But my father didn't agree, so it didn't end."

"Did he try to get you to touch him?"

"Yes, and it made me sick. It just thoroughly made me ill. He'd want me to kiss him there also. I—it would make me sick. I couldn't stand it."

"He started out by wanting you to kiss him, or just to touch him?"

"He never—when I was very young, I wanted to know what he looked like, so I investigated.* And he just lay down, and let me look. And I believe why it sickened me so—I don't know why I didn't tell it before, I was used to walking into the bathroom when he was going to the bathroom. And it just sickened me, to think—I don't know, that I would kiss him in the same way he kissed me. I could never do it. I'd try because I knew it pleased him, but I just couldn't."

"You didn't really like to kiss him there."

"I hated it. Because it didn't mean anything to me. It wasn't sex; it was a game. I couldn't see any point in it. What's the use? I didn't want to do it. If he wanted to do it, he could do it, but I didn't want to."

"To you it was a game."

"Yes. Only a game—it was a fun game."

"But it had some significance to his kissing you on the mouth."

"I don't understand."

"There was a reason why—that if he had not kissed you on the vagina, if you were not playing this game, that you would not have minded him kissing you on the lips."

---

* It should be recognized by the reader that the child is also curious. It is this curiosity that many psychiatrists and psychologists interpret as the seductiveness of the child. But one has to differentiate between the responsibility of an adult and of a child. Despite curiosity, it is interesting to note the innate revulsion toward the incestuous act.

"I don't know. I've never liked anyone—well, even when I was dating, I couldn't stand anyone to kiss me on the mouth. It just—I don't know, it means too much to me. It's—I don't like an aggressive love. I like a gentle love. Spring days and this kind of love, not hard, cold love. I don't like it. I can't stand aggressive men. I hate them. I feel like I'm being mauled, and I'd probably kill one if he ever tried it."

"Kissing other men disturbs you. Have there been other boys or men, since you've left your father's home, who have kissed you on the vagina?"

"Uh-huh."

"Is this something that you seek?"

"No. To me it's always seemed very strange, almost perverted. But, yet, I don't enjoy sex—just intercourse. I would rather—I get more enjoyment out of just being close to someone than I do out of the sex act. I get nothing out of that but a sickening feeling, to the point of going into the bathroom and being sick. It does nothing for me."

"Do you know why that is?"

"No, not really. It bothers me because I know that it's not wrong. And I love so much to be able to give. If a man wouldn't take me, I would give. But I can't stand thinking I'm being taken because I'm not that kind of girl. I'll give, and I'll give completely, but I will not be taken. I think that's why Bob and I could get along. He was very unaggressive; he was almost passive. I could give to him. He wasn't taking it from me. That's something I can't stand."

"How often did you and your father engage in this play?"

"Maybe five times a week."

"Do you think that you became insensitive to it? It must have become a day-to-day, sort of a nothing-type of feeling."

"Yes, with him. Then I decided to go out and experiment."

"How old were you?"

"The first time that I ever engaged in any kind of

sexual activity with another man I was fifteen, but it was a real bummer, you know. It didn't have any meaning past the fact that I found out that other guys were built the same way my father was. Then I was told that I couldn't have children, and it made me determined that I would have one—married or not. It bothered me deeply that I couldn't. But yet, I couldn't go through with sex. I don't know whether I figured the stork was going to bring it, or what, but I couldn't go through with sex. I developed a reputation of being a tease because I just couldn't go through with it when it came right down to it."

"You couldn't have children?"

"No. I caught some kind of disease."

"How did you get the disease? Do you know?"

"Yeah. I got it from my father's gums. But I found out since I can have kids."

"As a child, did you ever masturbate?"

"Yes. I think I did."

"Tell me about it."

"My father was gone. We were sent off the island because the Red Chinese were invading it, and they had to get all dependents off. My father stayed there and we came back to the States and he didn't come back for a few months. So, of course I missed this. I grew dependent on it and I started experimenting. I knew what he did and I figured maybe I could do it myself. But it wasn't the same thing."

"Have you ever had a climax?"

"Yes, I have."

"Can you remember the first time?"

"Yes, because I've only climaxed once."

"Could you tell me about that?"

"I was stoned on acid and I don't know whether I climaxed from sex or I climaxed from the acid. I really don't know. I was with a guy who was a pusher, and he was on speed.* He was very fast. Everything was fast, but he was, I must admit, very good in bed. I was very

---

* Speed is methedrine, a liquid stimulant that many teen-agers inject into veins in various parts of the body.

inhibited. He knew about the problem that I had had, so he started talking to me. And he really just kind of went through my whole life from the beginning to the end. But I never said what happened. I mean, I didn't explain it in the same way I am now. He asked me what I had been involved in. I told him. He said, 'Well let's try it.' And I said, 'Okay, groovy, let's try it.' I believe I climaxed then."

"Let's try what?"

"Anything. He'd say. 'Did your dad do this?' I'd say, 'Yes.' And he'd say, 'Okay, let's us try it.' I mean, it was a groovy relationship. I was very, very hung up on him. He was—oh, action. That's the only word to explain him. He was like a clown. He was happy all the time. He never was unhappy. And he could make me laugh when nobody else could."

"He didn't make you feel as though it were bad."

"He made it beautiful. He'd say, 'Okay, the room's going to change colors now, and it's going to be groovy.' And he'd tell me what color, and suddenly the whole room was the color. Like somebody had taken a bucket of paint and thrown it into the room and it just spread over the walls and the air itself, and it would just change colors like that. It was beautiful. It was the most beautiful thing I have ever been involved in. It was fabulous."

"You got your mind off yourself."

"Completely. I completely relaxed. I was completely involved in what I was doing, and happily so. And I was giving and he was giving and there was no taking involved."

"But ordinarily, you're not relaxed?"

"No."

"Why is that?"

"Because I feel like I'm being taken, and I don't like it. Because the guy will be passive to a point, a manly point, of course. And then he just can't be."

"Then what happens?"

"It just turns me off. I can't stand it. I feel like I'm being mauled and pawed and I don't dig it. I don't dig it. I don't like sex to be like an animal. And that's all it is with most men that I've met. It's an animalistic instinct, and I think it can be much more than that.

"You felt that way toward Bob?"

"He was very—he was passive and then he was aggressive. Frighteningly aggressive. He wanted me to talk about it. I couldn't talk about it."

"Talk about what?"

"What was happening in my mind when we were involved in sex. I couldn't talk about it. I didn't know what I was supposed to say. I couldn't understand what—you know. And he said I didn't react. I would physically, but I couldn't talk to him about it. I don't think you're supposed to talk to them about it. I'd talk afterward and before, but not during."

"Did you ever have intercourse with your father?"

"He attempted it, but I'm very, very small. It hurt so much that I never let him."

"How old were you when your father attempted to have intercourse with you?"

"Eight."

"I would like you to tell me about it."

"No."

"Why not?"

"I don't want to talk about it. I don't want to think about it."

"Can Cindy tell me about it?"

Barbara sat, her eyes closed, for several moments. I asked her again, "Can Cindy tell me about the time her father tried to have intercourse with her?"

Barbara stirred, descended into a deeper sleep, and then, in the high-pitched voice of a child, said, "Cindy and her daddy were playing the game. Cindy was lying there, doing nothing, like she always did when they played the game. Then her daddy looked up from kissing her and he kind of shifted his body up, and then he reached up and put his hands under her *tushee*. Then he kind of pulled her down underneath him. Cindy said to her daddy, 'Daddy, what are you doing?'

"And her daddy said, 'You're going to like this, honey.' Cindy didn't know what her daddy was doing, but her daddy said to her, 'It's another way to play the game love.' And Cindy said, 'All right, daddy.' And then Cindy's daddy tried to put his tinkle into her tinkle. But it hurt Cindy. It hurt her. It hurt her very much. And she said, 'Daddy, that hurts me.' And her daddy said to her, 'It will just hurt for a moment, but then you'll like it.' But Cindy didn't like it. It hurt so bad. She began to cry, she began to cry very loud. And she said, 'Please, daddy, stop.' And finally Cindy's daddy stopped. He didn't try to put his tinkle into her tinkle anymore that day."

"Did your father attempt any other type of sexual relations with you?"

"What kind?"

"Anal intercourse, beatings, urination?"

"No, but he did take photos of us together."

"When did that start?"

"When I was twelve."

"Tell me about that."

"At first they were just of me, and then he wanted to get into them. And he'd take them of very perverted scenes. They were just sickening."

"They were perverted?"

"Yes. He'd take a picture of me kissing him—you know, kissing him there. Stuff like that."

"And how did you feel about it?"

"I hated it. It was like a stag movie. It was sickening. It made me feel dirty, low, just like a slut. I couldn't believe that he would have me do something like that."

"Yet you did it."

"He asked me to."

"Is that the only reason?"

"Uh-huh. And he would be nice to me if I would go along with him."

"How would he be nice to you?"

"He wouldn't hassle me. If I got bad grades—big deal. If I got in trouble—big deal. If I was late coming home, so what."

"And what would he do if you tried to resist?"
"I would get in trouble for things I didn't even do."
"He would hassle you then?"
"Yeah."
"But you also blackmailed him, you said. How would you do that?"
"Well, like I wanted to go on a trip to see the Beatles with the YMCA, and I didn't have the money. I knew about the trip months in advance and didn't bother to earn the money. I was lazy and spoiled, and so I told him he'd either give me the money and talk mom into letting me have it without hassling me about it, or I would tell her about us. So he gave me the money. And then I told him I was only kidding anyhow. But, I wasn't kidding; I was serious. And when I wanted to use the car or stay home from school, if he wouldn't let me, I'd be mean to him."
"How would you be mean to him?"
"He'd try to touch me, and I'd tell him to get away from me. I'd tell him he made me sick."
"How did he react to that?"
"It hurt him."
"How did it make you feel when. . . ."
"Like shit. I mean you feel terrible to do something like that."
"Did it give you a sense of power?"
"No. It made me sick. I never, never want to control anyone like that. It's too much pain. Too much pain. And I got the worst of the deal, because I had to think about what I'd done."
"That would make you feel ill, would it?"
"Oh, God. I couldn't believe what I'd done. I can't believe now the things I did. It just seems unreal to me, but I know I did it."
"What other types of pictures did he take?"
"Oh, very—what I feel are obscene poses of me. I didn't mind him taking them if they were decent-looking, you know. Because I wasn't that ashamed of myself. But when they were obscene, I just. . . ."

A CASE HISTORY OF INCEST

"I'm not sure I understand what you mean by obscene."

"Direct poses. I'd rather not say the words."

"You've heard the words before."

"I know it, but. . . ."

"He took direct snapshots of your vagina."

"Stuff like that."

"What would he do with the pictures?"

"Hide them, and look at them. It was strange. He didn't like—like *Playboy* Magazine, the girls in them— He didn't like anything like that. It was just me. And I must admit, I'm just not that great. I mean, I'm not all that bad, but I'm not that great."

"Why do you think he selected you?"

"I really don't know. It's completely stupid because at the age he selected me, there just wasn't too much to look at. I really don't know."

"Would he spend time examining you?"

"Yes."

"And how did you feel about that?"

"Embarrassed. Completely humiliated and embarrassed. I felt like I was on the stage."

"Would he do this often?"

"No, not often, but enough to bother me. And I have two moles on my rear end. They're on the—I've been told they're very well placed. They embarrass me to pieces because if I wear a bikini or anything, which I do wear, someone's always commenting. They're not very big or anything—I don't know, they're just well placed and they embarrass me. And he used to always say, 'You've got the cutest ass in town,' or something like that. It would just thoroughly embarrass me."

"Did he seem to resent that you would not kiss him?"

"No. I just usually made a joke about it or something. And anytime I want to get out of anything, I make a joke."

"Did he ever have a climax?"

"One time he did, and it sickened me completely. It just—ugh. I think I said, 'What have you done?' It just completely blew my mind. I couldn't believe it. I had never . . . I didn't even know that happened." Barbara smiled and then giggled.

"About how old were you then?"

"Ummm. Eleven."

"When he had the climax, what was he doing?"

"Kissing me, you know—there."

"And you felt sickened."

"Oh, God. I couldn't believe it. It mortified me."

"When you think—when you're having intercourse now, now that you're older, do you ever think of what a man is like when he is having a climax?"

"I wonder. I don't think about it. I wonder about it. I wonder what it's like. I wonder what goes through their head. And then, they get an animal look on their face, and I start crying, and I usually push them away. It sickens me; I can't stand the animal look on anybody."

"What does that remind you of?"

"I don't think people are animals. I don't think they ought to look like animals. That's the whole thing. Love and sex are a beautiful thing. I don't think you ought to be an animal when you do it."

"When you're having relations with a boy or a man now, you want him to be passive. There comes a time, however, when they start kissing you, say on your breasts. What sort of feelings do you have now when you're kissed on your breasts?"

"I enjoy it."

"But. . . ."

"But, nothing. I enjoy it."

"You enjoy having your body kissed."

"Uh-huh. Yeah."

"When do you get the feeling that it is animal-like?"

"It's when the intercourse begins. The guy gets all hot and bothered and acts like an animal. He looks like an animal."

"There's something about his looks. The look on his face."

"His eyes."

"His eyes? What does that remind you of?"

"My father."

"What would your father be doing when he got this look on his face?"

"Kissing me. And then he'd look up like I was supposed to say, 'Oh, goody, goody. I'm sure glad you're doing that.' But I never would. And then he'd say, 'Do you enjoy it?' And I wouldn't answer him."*

"What would you think of your father at that point?"

"I wanted to kill him."

"Why?"

"Because he looked like an animal. A low, dirty, filthy animal. I can't stand it."

"You know why you feel he was an animal at that point. That was because he was kissing you."

"I don't think so. It's the look in his face like the time he beat me."

"Oh? Tell me about that."

"My best girlfriend—I was going to testify for that guy, Buddy, on the narcotics case—well, my best girlfriend, Rozelle, had been living with us for like a year and she found out and told my parents that I was testifying against the narcotics agent in order to have his license revoked—which was not true. Anyhow, without giving me a chance to explain, my mother literally beat me to the floor. I kept begging her not to hit me anymore. Then my father came over and started beating me. They both looked like animals wanting to hurt me—wanting me to die. And my mother kept screaming, 'You have a sister! What are you trying to do—have everybody sell her dope?' I tried to explain but they wouldn't listen. They just kept hitting me and hitting me. They believed Rozelle, that damned bitch! I begged them, 'Please let me go to my bedroom.' But every time I got up my father would kick me. It seemed like it went on for hours, and finally—I got them to let me go to my room. Then the next day my folks left on vacation and I had to go to school because

*This, of course, explains why she hated to talk with her husband during intercourse.

my sister was having some problems. My mom never had time for Holly. So I kind of mothered her and took care of her and made sure her grades were good and everything. Anyhow, I went to the school to talk to her teacher and I took Rozelle with me and I drove my parents' car. And I told Rozelle, 'I'll be about an hour. You can go get a Coke, if you want; take the car and come back.' I was only gone about a half an hour but she didn't come back and I had to walk about four miles in the heat in heels and a dress. So, when I got home I said, 'That wasn't too cool.' And she came at me and started beating me and yelling at me."

"Who was beating you?"

"Rozelle. She just kept hitting me and hitting me. I couldn't stop her. I begged her not to hit me anymore. I was going out of my mind. I finally got away from her and ran to my momma's bedroom, hoping she'd be there—hoping for once she'd be there and do something to help me. But she was gone, so I crawled—and I was like a small child trying to cover myself up with something that smelled like my mother. Her bed. Her blankets. Her sheets. Anything."

"Why was Rozelle beating you?"

"I don't know. I really don't know. She just kept saying, 'You can do this to your parents, but you're not going to do this to me.' "

"Do what to your parents?"

"I don't know. I was telling her that it wasn't a good scene to leave me there without my car. And she wasn't insured or anything. If there was a wreck, I'd be blamed. And it wasn't a good scene. She really shouldn't have done it. And I wasn't mad, I was just explaining to her. I wasn't even raising my voice, and she just came at me. She looked like—I want to kill you, Barbara. I want you to die right here."

"Now when you think of an animal look, and you think of the looks on your parents when they were beating you—is that more animal to you, or the look of your father when he's kissing you?"

A CASE HISTORY OF INCEST 61

"It was the same look. The same emotional buildup. The same frenzied look."

"Ah, your father was frenzied as he was kissing you."

"Yes." And Barbara suddenly began to sob.

"I want you to relax ... that's a girl ... take a deep breath, Barbara. You're all right. Relax your hands, relax your entire body. Have you ever had any homosexual experiences?"

"One time a dyke tried to pick me up and I jumped out of the car."

"Why?"

"That's not my bag. I've been through enough perversion without that."

"You think of it as a perversion."

"Yes. I believe so. At least for me. I think everyone has their own thing. For some people, it's not a perversion. For them—do your own thing, you know. But for me it is a perversion. Therefore I don't care to participate, and if I don't care to participate in something, I don't. That's a person's prerogative. I know a lot of queer men. They're good friends of mine. They're really heavy people, and they dig me because I have no prejudice. They sit and try to make it with a guy and I couldn't care less, because if the guy's going to do it, that's his thing. I probably would never have sex with him again, but if that's his thing, he can do it."

"Why wouldn't you have sex with him again?"

"I don't know, it's just a thing. I can't say definitely because I don't really know that I wouldn't. It would all depend on the situation."

"I have a feeling, a very strong feeling, that there is part of you that feels that sex is pretty dirty."

"Well, like the animal thing. That's the only thing that makes it dirty to me. I don't think people ought to be like animals."

"I wonder if you might not feel like an animal if you started to have a climax."

"I do. I reject a climax."

"Because?"

"Because that's like an animal. I don't want to look like they look at me."

"I see. Now, Barbara, at one point you told me you got a tremendous kick out of a nice trip, beautiful beads and flashing brilliant colors. I want you to see them again, as you begin another trip. You're dropping acid and it's going through your body. It's taking time, but it's seeping through. It's a magnificent trip, a beautiful trip. You're completely free, completely uninhibited. Your thoughts are grooving. You're going back, back, back into your childhood. And everything will become clear. I'm going to count slowly now. When I reach three, you'll be in the middle of the trip. The acid's going through you. You're feeling better and better even now. One. The acid's relaxing you. Relax. Your mind is expanding. Two. You're uninhibited. You're going deeper and deeper into your subconscious. You can talk about your past through Cindy. Three. You're going back, back, back. The lights are flashing and you're surrounded by color, warm, glowing color. Cindy's just a girl now. We're going to replay the scene, the first scene when Cindy was kissed. We're going to take Cindy back. I want you to think of a drum. It's going around and around. It's going back in time. Back in time and it's just before everything was going to start that day. Cindy was some place. I don't know whether it happened when Cindy was in the bathroom or in the bedroom or where. Just before it happened, in some way or another, her father got her attention. You're going to describe how Cindy's father looked."

Barbara's face took on the masklike appearance that is so characteristic of the deepest somnambulistic state of hypnosis. A little girl spoke.

"Cindy's changing her clothes. It's morning. Momma went to the market. Daddy said, 'Cindy, what are you doing?' 'I'm getting dressed, daddy.' Her daddy picks her up and sits her down on the bed. She has a bunk bed. She sleeps on the top because she's a big girl now. Daddy puts her on her back. He kisses her on the

A CASE HISTORY OF INCEST 63

tummy. Daddy looks hungry. Cindy doesn't understand why he doesn't get something to eat. But it doesn't seem to be that kind of hunger. So Cindy sits and he hugs her. 'Daddy, what are we going to do today?' 'Daddy's going to take care of my little girl.' 'We're going to play house, daddy?' 'No, we're not going to play house.' 'What are we going to do?' 'We're going to play love.' 'Daddy, what's love?' Then daddy kisses her and he gets up and he says, 'That's love.' Cindy doesn't understand how that could be love. Daddy just kissed her. Mommy kisses her sometimes. Does mommy love her, too? Cindy doesn't really know. Daddy wants to play some more. It's a fun game, but it tickles, and Cindy doesn't like to be tickled. So she says, 'Daddy, that tickles, please don't tickle.' But her daddy goes ahead and he starts moving all over, Cindy thinks maybe, maybe he has to go to the bathroom. Cindy moves around a lot when she has to go to the bathroom. But she really doesn't know. Daddy keeps playing. He keeps kissing her and kissing her. Not on her tummy. He kisses her where she goes to the bathroom. Cindy thinks that's dirty. Her mommy said you should never touch that. Only with the toilet paper and the washrag. Cindy says, 'Daddy, you shouldn't do that. Only with toilet paper and mommy says you shouldn't touch it.' Daddy says, 'That's okay, that's how you play love.' Then her mommy came home. Cindy sits up, 'Mommy's home. Mommy's going to play, too.' Daddy says, 'No, Cindy. This is a secret.' Cindy doesn't understand what a secret means. Daddy says, 'You just don't tell anybody. Not anybody. Not even mommy.' Cindy says, 'Not even mommy?' He says, 'Not mommy.' So Cindy thinks this is a fun game. Daddy goes out and Cindy gets finished dressing. She goes out and she whispers in daddy's ear, 'Let's play some more.' Daddy says, 'We can't play now.' Cindy doesn't understand. Then Sally comes over and Cindy goes to play. She plays all day. She has lots of fun. But Cindy can't quit thinking about daddy's game. It was more fun. She comes home in the afternoon and she says, 'Daddy, can we play some more?

Mommy's gone again.' So daddy says, 'Yes, we can play some more now.' And he takes Cindy into the bedroom—to mommy's bedroom. Cindy's not allowed to play in mommy's bedroom. So she says, 'Daddy, we can't play in mommy's bedroom, mommy said so.' Daddy says, 'That's okay. It's my bedroom, too.' So daddy plays some more. Only this time he lays down on the bed, too. Cindy doesn't do anything. She thinks it's kind of a dumb game because she doesn't get to do anything but just lay there. But it feels good. It makes her feel good all over, so she plays the game. And daddy says, 'Come on, we've got to get up now.' Cindy doesn't want to quit playing. Cindy wants to play the game all the time. But she gets up because she does what daddy says. That's being a good girl. Then daddy gets Cindy up at night to go to the bathroom. Cindy wants to play again. She always wants to play the game. She always asks daddy to play the game, but only when mommy's not around because Cindy found out she can't play the game when mommy's home. Only at night. When mommy sleeps."

"Fine. Now we are going to turn the memory drum around and around. We're going to go to the time when Cindy is curious about what daddy looks like. What made Cindy curious and how did it all start?"

"Mommy was gone and daddy was taking a shower. Cindy saw daddy walk from the linen closet to the shower in his underpants. But he had a funny thing out front. Cindy didn't have one. Stu and Jimmy had one, that's Cindy's brothers, but it wasn't like that. It wasn't the same. So daddy was in the shower, and Cindy knocked on the door. 'Daddy, can I come in?' Daddy didn't say anything for a minute, then he said, 'Come on in, honey.' Cindy went in and daddy didn't have any clothes on. She was scared. She walked up and asked him what it was, and daddy didn't answer. Cindy asked again, 'Daddy, what is it? What do you do with it?' And daddy said, 'I go to the bathroom with it.' And Cindy looked down and she didn't have one. 'Daddy, why don't I have one?' 'Because you're a girl.' 'Why don't I get to have one?' 'Because you're a girl and girls aren't supposed to have one.' Cindy didn't understand, but that was all right, because she didn't understand very much. She said, 'Daddy, are we going to play some more?' He said, 'Yes. We'll play some more.' So they went into the bedroom. Cindy wanted to look. Cindy wanted to see what it looked like, so she asked daddy if she could. And he said, 'Okay.' Cindy thought it was funny. It looked funny. It looked really funny. She laughed and she giggled and daddy thought it was cute and he hugged her. Cindy liked to be hugged. Then they played some more."

"Let the drum take you back a little further, Barbara, and recreate the time when daddy first asked Cindy to kiss him. How old was Cindy then?"

"Seven."

"What was she doing?"

"Daddy was playing with Cindy."

"The same game?"

"Yeah. Only daddy pushed Cindy's mouth down to that thing. Cindy didn't know what she was supposed to do, so she just looked at him. Her daddy said, 'Kiss it.' So she kissed it, but it didn't seem to be the kind of kiss that he wanted. And daddy said, 'Put it in your mouth.' Cindy said, 'Oooh, I can't do that.' And daddy kind of got mad, so Cindy did. It made Cindy so sick. She couldn't get over it. It made her so sick. Why was her daddy making her do this? She didn't understand. She didn't like that part of the game. She didn't want to play the game anymore. She didn't like the game."

"Did she keep playing it because daddy insisted?"

"Cindy acted like she was going to get sick, like she was going to throw up, so daddy stopped, but daddy went ahead and played the same game."

"And he never had Cindy kiss him there again?"

"He did it all the time, but Cindy always acted like she was going to get sick, so daddy would stop. She knew daddy would stop if she acted like she was going to be sick."

"And when Cindy grew up and got older, did she ever like that part of the game?"

"When she got married, but not any other time."

"Now, Barbara, I want you to go into a deeper, deeper sleep. We've had a very exhausting session, and I want you to rest before I awaken you. And again, when I awaken you, you will not remember anything you've said while under hypnosis. Now relax, and sleep."

A Telephone Call,

NOVEMBER 17

My answering service called during lunch hour to tell me that Barbara had called and left a message to call her back. I called, and in a matter of moments Barbara was telling me she wanted to quit her job. I asked if there was any particular reason why she wanted to quit at that moment, and she said she was just totally fed up with the routine, mundane, chimpanzee work that was required of her. I suggested that she not quit her job until we had at least had another meeting.

Before the appointment I had set with her for the next day, I decided to look again at the copious notes I had made during our first two meetings. After reading through them thoroughly two or three times, I found myself fascinated with a direction the sessions had taken.

The treatment of a psychopath is not particularly rewarding in terms of effecting a cure. Unconsciously I was anticipating failure. Nor did I always completely believe what she told me, but more importantly, I did not necessarily believe her feelings. As a consequence I found myself hammering away at each point in her history, examining each detail mercilessly to tease out the feelings and magnify them. I had to build on those human emotions that are characteristically absent in a psychopath. By regressing her in this fashion, I was essentially effecting a rebirth. The bricks (the contents of her life) were the same, but the mortar (the emotions that bound the bricks together) was different. Her feelings as she relived her experience became stronger and more real.

Her revelations reflected the tumultuous conflicts of love and hate that boiled within her. The feelings she had for her parents were both confused and intense. Her call seeking my reaction to quitting her job was the beginning of the transference phenomenon. She would soon start to respond to me as a father figure, hopefully in a healthier way than with her own father. I found myself becoming more optimistic about her recovery. I decided to continue treatment in the same vein. The material she imparted on the good LSD trip certainly proved fruitful. I wondered what a bad trip would yield. I was to find out the following afternoon.

Fourth Visit,

NOVEMBER 18

For the first time, Barbara was about five minutes late for our appointment but seemed eager and ready to proceed with our hypnosis treatment. I suspected that resistance was developing and questioned her feelings about our sessions. She denied any negative feelings, but I knew better. I made a mental note to pursue it later, and prepared her for hypnosis.

I asked her to stare at the flashing design and began to count her to sleep. Within moments she relaxed, breathing deeply. Her brown eyes closed, and again she slipped into a somnifacient trance.

"Barbara, tonight we're going to take another trip. You're going to take a trip like you took once before, only this will be a bad trip. I want you to relive a bad trip and tell me about it. You took acid a short time ago. You're beginning to feel the effects. You can feel the effects more and more. It's getting worse. Worse. You can see it so clearly. Tell me what it's like."

Barbara shuddered, "Everything is very dry, so dry. The air is dry. The land is dry. The people are all dry. They don't have any moisture in them. They don't have any life in them. Everybody's dry. All the trees died. All the flowers died. Everything is dry except for me, me and Sharon's boyfriend, Frank. I don't understand. She's my best friend. They're going to be married, but he's so out of sight my mind won't let him dry up, just everybody else. When he touches something, it lives again, it doesn't die. We're gonna go for a walk—going to walk on the school ground. It's across the street. It's very dark outside, the moon is down. It's kind of cool, even for summer, it's very cool. We're dressed just alike, peacoats, bellbottom pants, and I think that's groovy. But everything's so dry. I can feel the air in me. It seems to try to dry me out too, but I won't let it. Frank doesn't feel it. He's above it all. So groovy a guy. I really dug him for a long time. Now we've got a chance to be together because Sharon is acting like a real ass. Frank doesn't want anything to do with her and he and I have been seeing each other while she's at work. Everybody seems to be on bummers tonight. We got bum acid—that's it, bum acid. The school ground is damp. It seems odd, because everything is so dry. But, yet, when I touch it, it's dry again. We decide to lie down on the ground. There was a guard watching the school, and Frank thinks he saw us, so we lay down flat because it's black, and there are trees behind us. But I hear things in the trees and I'm scared. There's a graveyard behind the trees. Frank starts saying scary things. People were getting up out of the graves and walking around, and I was scared. I want to go back, but Frank says we have to stay down because the guard'll call the cops. So we stayed down. But the guard gave up and left, and we thought that was funny. Then Frank tried to touch me, but I wouldn't let him. I thought, We'll make a game of it, like tag, and I started running around. But I could see those people in the graveyard walking around and I'm scared to run. I just want to lay down and hide. And, now, Frank even scares me. He was so groovy a minute ago—he was so groovy, and now he scares me. His face looked horrid, horrid—just like he has two bodies and they are splitting. One's blue, pale, see-through, ghostlike blue, and that seems to be the part of him I've never seen before. I don't like it. Everybody seems to be walking around with two bodies. One of them is material and one of them you can see through. So I said, "Let's go back. The cops are probably going to come if we don't get off the grounds because they've been picking people up for loitering.'

"So we go back to Sharon's house and it's a groovy house. It's always been groovy. It has all kinds of psychedelic things. All kinds of hash pipes and things, and you can use them if you want to. But suddenly it's like a funeral parlor, and I don't want to be there. I got on a real bummer. I was scared. I'd never been on a bummer before. I didn't like it. I said, 'This is bum acid—it's not really acid.' She said, 'It's real acid. I made it myself.' And I know she makes good acid. She said, 'What's bumming your trip?' And I can't tell her. I don't really know, except Sharon has always bummed my trip. I get tired of her. I hate her. I don't—I've never said I hated her before. I don't really hate her. I just hate things she does. The world seems to be very close around me. Too close, like I'm going to strangle. And Frank came out, and suddenly he was the way he was before, and it was really groovy. He wanted to know what was up, so I just told him flat out. I really liked him and I couldn't stand to see him around Sharon because she was such a bitch. She always treated guys bad and they never even knew it until it was over. And he wouldn't believe me. He just wouldn't believe me. Then I said, 'I want to go to bed.' So I went in and I went to bed. That was all there was, but I had nightmares. I had nightmares all night long. I don't like bum trips. I never want to have another."

"Tell me about your nightmares."

"When I first went in and went to bed, Frank came in and he said he'd cared about me a long time and he didn't think I cared about him. But I was afraid it was a line, and I didn't want to listen. I asked him to leave. Barry was there, and he really liked me. He came over all the time. My parents liked him. He was straight. He never took any dope, but he was still a groovy guy, you know. He grooved with us. Nobody pushed anybody to take dope. I mean, everybody took it because they wanted to. But everybody had taken orange wedges that night and everybody was on a bummer. It was really bad. The worst trip we'd ever gotten.

"Then I fell asleep. And all these people—Sharon was a lesbian. But all the guys, everybody there—there were so many people there, they all came in. I know I was asleep. I must have been asleep because it never would have happened like that. All the men were tearing at my clothes and the girls too. I couldn't believe what was happening. I was screaming, and screaming and screaming. I just wanted to wake up so bad, so bad. I didn't want to think about it anymore. I didn't want anything like that to come in my mind. And then Sharon came in and was shaking me, trying to wake me up and I was screaming. Everybody knew I was on a bummer. They knew it was the first one I'd ever been on. They were all scared because you can do some pretty freaky things on bummers. She brought me some hot tea. The kids grew the tea themselves and it's really groovy green tea. I told her that I wanted to go back to sleep. And I did.

"And in my sleep I went to heaven—only all there were were devils and they were walking around on the clouds breaking down the Golden Gates. They were tearing everything in heaven apart and taking the gold and going to earth and selling it. Gold in the streets. At one time everything was so beautiful, but the devils had taken over all of it and they were just tearing it apart. Then I woke up and stayed up the rest of the day."

I questioned her about the obvious lesbian-related parts of the dream that she had while on the trip, and she told me she had had one dream concerning lesbian tendencies previously. It had happened one night when she was in the seventh grade. A friend of hers, Carol, had spent the night at her home. Soon after Barbara had gone to sleep and had just dozed off, she felt Carol put her hand between her legs. Barbara awakened immediately and told her to "cool it." When she did go to sleep, she dreamt about women running around grasping at each other's breasts and at other parts of the body. But in the dream there were no actual sexual relations.

I asked her how long it had taken her to get off of her bummer. She told me she had dropped the acid about five o'clock and it always took her at least forty minutes to get started.

She said, "The first twenty minutes you can't eat anything. The second twenty minutes you can't go to the bathroom because it hasn't gone completely through your system and you can lose half the effects." She claimed that the trip was a bummer because the "stuff" had heroin in it.

"It had heroin in it?"

"Yeah," Barbara said, "Heroin can make you—unless you shoot it, it's a real bummer. It's not good stuff to take. Orange wedges are mescaline, heroin, methedrine, and a little bit of acid, not much. Usually they use Orange Ossly with it, because that's a good trip and the heroin sets it off. It gets a lot of speed in it and gives you a rush. But this rush was a bad rush. I don't know why it was such a bummer. Maybe the way it was put together or something. But everybody got on a bummer from it. The mescaline Sharon got had heroin in it and she didn't know it. We found out later."

"Was Sharon a chemist that she could make acid?"

"It's not hard to make. I used to watch her. It depends on what you want to make. I used to help her make hash. That stuff stinks—yuck. But acid, it took about fifteen minutes to stir up enough acid to get everybody in town zonked out of their head. We sure had a heavy time. I'd like to do it all over again. I miss that."

I learned that she had been living with Sharon from January to May of this year. Sharon was twenty-two years old and owned the house they lived in. I questioned her as to whether she had sexual feelings toward Sharon. She denied them and said that while she liked her, she liked Rozelle a great deal more. She also denied sexual feelings for Rozelle, stating that her love for Rozelle was only that of a sister. I asked her if she was afraid of this lesbian feeling within herself, and she said she was because of the way she felt about sex with men. She felt that her relationship with her father had disoriented her relationships with all other men.

I decided to find out more about her other family relationships and asked her about them. She had a younger sister, Holly, and two brothers, Jim and Stu. Stu was her senior by two years and both Holly and Jimmy were younger. Holly is fifteen and Jim is twelve. She described Stu as her "big, wonderful brother." They had always been close and he's always looked out for her and she for him. She said, "He's fantastic. I'm so proud of him."

I asked her if she thought Stu had ever suspected anything was going on between her and their father. She told me that she'd tried to tell him when she was fifteen but he wouldn't believe her. She had gone to him seeking help, but Stu rejected her by not believing what she said. She realized afterward that there was nothing he could really do, and she was sorry she'd mentioned it at all because she didn't want him to hate their dad.

I decided to examine her feelings about Stu's reaction more intently. I counted her into a deeper sleep and said, "Barbara, I want you to go back in time, back to when you are fifteen years old. You were thinking about telling your brother Stu about you and your dad. Tell me about it. You're fifteen years old. You're fifteen years old and you're going to tell your brother Stu about you and your dad."

Barbara began to mumble and I couldn't understand what she was saying. I put her into a still deeper sleep and again commanded her to describe the incident.

She began, "I was drunk. I came home and I said, 'Stu, I want to talk to you.' He was in bed. Mom and dad were gone for the weekend. So he sits up. He always got up and listened to me when I wanted to talk. Usually it was a pretty far-out and very interesting story 'cause it was usually a lie. I said. 'I think there's something you ought to know.' I was trying to be very grown-up about the whole thing. I said, 'Do you know what incest is?' And he says, 'No.' And I said, 'Well, I'll tell you.' I think he figured I'd just learned a new word. Anyhow, I proceeded to try to tell him and he said, 'You've got a great imagination, Barbie, but I just don't want to hear it.'"

"I want you to relive the part and tell me exactly what you told him. 'I know what incest is....' What did you tell him?"

"I said, 'Well, Stu, dad and I have had incest since I was very, very young.' And that's when he said it. I mean, that was as far as I got. He didn't want to hear it."

"Did you explain to him what incest was?"

"Yeah. I said, 'It's relations between family members.'"

"You just said relations or did you say sexual relations?"

"I just said relations. At the time, I couldn't even say sex."

"You couldn't even say sex then. Where had you been the night that you had gotten high?"

"Over at Rozelle's house. Her mom and dad were always gone, always. And they always had something in the cabinet. Anyhow, we used to take her mom's whiskey and fill the bottle with water. You know, fill up what we drank. But I didn't like it.... Yuck. It was an ugly taste."

"Tell me about Rozelle."

"She was built just like a boy and people thought of her like that. She could cuss with the best of them and she did. She was completely uninhibited. She'd get right down with the rest of them in the mud, and I couldn't do that. I wanted to be a girl—not a boy. Anyhow, so guys liked me because I was a girl. I represent girl and I didn't care if they knew it. Every time she got a boyfriend, I'd end up taking him away from her and it really put me on a bummer because she was my best friend and I didn't intend to do it. It just happened like that."

"How would Rozelle get right down in the mud with the boys?"

"The way they'd talk. I mean—I hate to say the words, but she'd come up and say, 'Hey, fuck you, bastard.' Just like that to some guy she hardly even knew."

"How would that make you feel?"

"Oh, God. It'd make me feel sick. The guys—I'd talk to them and they'd say, 'God, Barbie, I'm glad you're not like that.' I always thought the guys all liked her, and the more I got to know the guys, the more I realized they couldn't have, you know. She was a guy, she wasn't a girl."

"Tell me some more about your feelings about her being a guy and not a girl."

"Well, I just mean in the way she talked and—you're trying to make it sound like I thought about her sexually. I didn't. She turned me off cold."

"I was wondering, though, if that went through your mind."

"Never."

"Had she had sexual relations?"

"We had them the same night."

"You mean you and she had sex at the same time? But you'd had sexual relations before that, hadn't you?"

"Yeah. But with my father."

"I see. How old were you then, the first time you had sex with somebody other than your father?"

"I was fifteen."

"Did you and Rozelle discuss having sexual relations together?"

"Well, she was so naive it wasn't even funny. I mean, that girl had no idea of nothing. She absolutely didn't have any idea of what was going on. I've never met anybody so naïve and dumb in my entire life. She must never have taken biology or anything. She'd come to me with the weirdest, way-out questions about sex. And it seemed so dumb that I would be telling her about it because I was much younger. But she depended on me because she wasn't very bright. She had a lot of potential at being bright, but she wasn't. Anyhow, the night we got drunk—I was with Tony and Rozelle, she was with Dave, this guy she'd been going with for a year and a half or so. Anyhow, it was so funny, because Tony and I were in one bedroom and she and Dave were in the other bedroom. And all of the sudden she comes running in and she says, 'Come here, come here,' a typical little-kid action. Two girls get together and discuss something while the guys sit in the bedroom, you know. I go over and I say, 'What the hell do you want?' She says, 'I can't tell you. I can't tell you.' And so she goes running back into the bedroom and this went on all night.

"So, finally, when the guys left, it was about six o'clock in the morning, she came in and she goes, 'I gotta tell you.' I said, 'Well, tell me.' She says, 'He screwed me.' I go, 'Well, so? What did you expect to happen? You're both drunk, what the hell do you expect?' It was really funny. She goes, 'Well, what happened with you?' I told her basically what the whole evening was about because we were both—she and Dave weren't as drunk as Tony and I. We were just, oh, shoot, messed up. Our heads were nothing. But I didn't tell her that I didn't want to do it. I couldn't tell her that part. I don't know why, pride, or what. Or the superior way she'd made me feel. I couldn't give it up. But, she was scared that she was pregnant and a million and one other things. After that she said, 'I will never, never, never, ever do anything like that again in my life.' And, so, I found out later she was doing it like every other week with somebody new. And this tore me apart because I trusted her. I trusted what she said was true, and she was a liar."

"What was your experience? You said that you were pretty drunk."

"Uh-huh. I was terribly, terribly drunk. Neither of us wanted to do it. In fact, we didn't even actually do it. He was so drunk he couldn't have, and I was so drunk, I didn't want to. I wanted to go to sleep."

"How did you know that he didn't want to?"

"I didn't say he didn't want to, I said he couldn't. We were both so drunk, we just wanted to sleep."

"I thought you said you had sexual relations, though, the first time that night."

"Well, I'd say we got the closest—we got as close as could be without actually going through the whole bit. He didn't come. That's the whole thing. We did have sexual relations, but he did not come."

"I see. Now originally when you started out, you had made plans to have Tony and Dave over. Tell me about that."

"Well, see, Roz's mom was divorced. She was dating the guy she's now married to, and they went to visit his relatives. Anyhow, I told my mom and dad I was going to spend the night with Roz because she was afraid to stay by herself. This was cool and they went along with it. So, we got over to Roz's and the boys were due about eight o'clock. Well, they got there all right, and they brought about four cases of beer. She and I had already mixed up this drink out of wine and whiskey and Coke and cherries and all kinds of junk. It was pretty good though. We strained it and put it in the refrigerator with crushed ice, and you know, it was really funny. It was good. Anyhow, we'd had three or four of these things before they got there, so we were pretty gone by then. What we had planned on was going to be a nice evening. We were going to go to a dance, and then maybe we'd come back and do our little thing. It was going to be really a groovy night. It never ended up that way though. I ended up taking a bath. I took three baths."

"Do your little thing? What do you mean by that?"

"Well, Roz and I had both figured we were going to find out what it was all about."

"Then you were planning it."

"Yeah. But the boys weren't because up until this time each of us had been dating these two guys, me like six or eight months, Roz for a year or two, and they knew we wouldn't do anything. But we had decided. Anyhow, I ended up taking three bubble baths, and we cooked French fried onion rings and ate bananas and ham and cold turkey. You know, a bunch of stupid things.

"Anyhow, I was taking these baths and I was thinking nobody can see me because I'm covered with bubbles, only there weren't any bubbles because they had all popped, and Tony and Dave and Roz were standing there talking to me and it was so dumb because I didn't have a bubble on me. But, for some reason, I wasn't embarrassed, and I usually was. I mean, I even got embarrassed in a pair of shorts. So, we ended up never going to the dance. Dave and Roz got into a fight and he threw her down on the furnace and burned her rear end. It was one of those grills on the floor and she burned little square screen marks on her rear end."

"Was she naked?"

"Yes." Barbara giggled.

"You got undressed. . . . ?"

"No. Tony and I went into the bedroom then and watched television and Dave and Roz stayed out in the living room."

"Did you have your clothes on when you went into the bedroom?"

"No, I had been through three baths by that time."

"Did Tony have his clothes on?"

"Yeah. It was a screwy evening, though; God that was fun."

"You were watching television and what happened?"

"Well, I started getting close to him, and he thought it was kind of strange, because I just never did. I kissed him and then, of course, he kissed me back and we didn't watch television anymore." Barbara laughed embarrassedly. ". . . . It's so crude. I hate to even say it, but Tony said, 'Ah . . . you know. I can't even get a hard-on.' I didn't even know what that was, but I agreed with him, you know. That's why the evening was such a bust. It was such a big nothing, but it was fun. I don't regret a minute of it. It was a blast."

"You were both naked lying on the bed, watching television. . . ."

"He wasn't naked."

"... But you were."

"Yeah. But I had a sheet over me."

"He had seen you in the bubble bath and you had gotten up naked and walked to the bedroom."

"No. I made him leave the room before I got up because the bubbles were covering me when I was in the tub, or so I thought."

"Were you drunk then?"

"Oh, God, yes."

"Okay, so you got in there, got under the sheets, and he came in."

"Right."

"And he had his clothes on."

"Yeah. He had on a blue turtleneck, a green pair of Levi's and a black pair of shoes and black socks. And he was very handsome."

"What did he look like?"

"He had beautiful black hair and the biggest blue eyes you've ever seen in your entire life. God, he's handsome."

"And how old was he?"

"He was twenty-three."

"Okay, so you were lying in bed, watching television, and you moved over and kissed him."

"Uh-huh. I kissed him on the mouth. We were laying there looking at each other, stoned on our asses, and just looking at each other with this stupid grin on our face, you know, and it was so dumb, so dumb, because the sheet got in the way, and the blankets got in the way, and Roz collected stuffed animals and they were all on the bed. You kind of had to move around and fit in between them as best you can because you throw them on the floor and Roz'd kill you. So, the animals were in the way and it was just a complete bummer. As far as a sex experience, it wasn't."

"How did you feel when he was touching you?"

"Drunk."

"Was that all?"

"Uh-huh."

"There wasn't any sensation?"

"Oh, scared. That was about it. I'd never been with a guy in my whole life."

"Did he touch you?"

"Yes. On the vagina, on the breasts, and on my rear end."

"Did it excite you at all?"

"No."

"Did you touch him?"

"No."

"Why not?"

"I just couldn't bring myself to. I tried, I really tried to get myself to want to, but I couldn't do it."

"I think it's important to you to know why you couldn't touch him. Tell me why."

"I really—I don't know, I guess because of my dad. I think I was afraid he was going to force me to do something I didn't want to do."

"What were you afraid he was going to force you to do?"

"Go down on him."

"That had entered your mind?"

"Yes, but only for a moment. Then I figured, if I didn't touch him, he wouldn't think of it. So I didn't touch him."

"Were you afraid of getting pregnant?"

"No."

"Did he know about your father?"

"No, but Roz did."

"Oh?"

"Roz was the first one I told. Actually, I hardly had to tell her a word. She just figured it out. This has happened with several people who know my family well. They would end up telling me or asking me if it was true. That's how obvious it was to other people."

"But how did it come about?—your telling Roz. What did you say?"

"I said, 'Roz, I've got a problem I've got to talk over with you.' She said, 'Does it concern your father?' I said, 'Yes.' And from there on she did all the talking."

"What did she say?"

"She said, 'You and him got some kind of thing going?' And I said, 'Yes, something like that.' She asked me how long, and I said, 'I really don't know. Since I was little.' We didn't go much further, but she said, 'Anytime you need to talk about it, just give me a call.' She didn't really understand what had gone on, because at that age you wouldn't really think about what did go on. You would think immediately of intercourse. But that has never happened. I used to have Roz come over and be with me at night when my father was going to be there and my mother was going to be gone, or I'd go over there because I couldn't stand to be with him with no one else around."

"What would happen?"

"He wouldn't leave me alone."

"Would you try to get him to leave you alone?"

"Yeah."

"How?"

"I've slapped him. I've told him to go to hell. I've told him everything I could dream of, but it doesn't make any impression at all."

"What would he do?"

"He'd start to cry; he'd break up."

"Would he lie down? Would he sit down or..."

"He'd sit down, or just walk around, or whatever came into his head. Or, he'd get furious. Just blow up, mad, and he'd go in and slam his door and mumble to himself, and he would grab a book and start reading or he'd turn his television way up and he'd slam things around and bang things and break things. And I'd say, 'Cool it, daddy, it ain't getting you anywhere.' That's how I actually talked to him, you know. I was on the same level with him. He was no longer a father to be respected, so I didn't treat him with any respect, except in front of my mother and my brothers and sister. But when we were alone, I would just as soon tell him to go to hell as I would to get a cup of coffee or something. Because in that frame of mind his whole face—he would not be the same person."

"How would he look? Describe him."

"He's a small man. He's not big. Well, he's not big; he's not small. He's five-eight. His face would get—I don't know—wider. And his eyebrows would come closer together and his nose would become broader. His mouth—his bottom lip would seem to blend into his chin, not be so much an exact line. And it was very strange because you couldn't actually see these changes. Even his hair would become more bristly. It was the strangest thing I had ever seen."

"Would he become quieter or more restless in this manner?"

"He'd become very quiet. I mean, quiet but restless. I don't know how—not talking, moving around, but he'd be like a cat. You wouldn't hear him, and you'd turn around and suddenly he was behind you."

"Doing what?"

"Just behind you. You wouldn't hear him come up."

"But you had a feeling he was behind you?"

"Yeah. I'd know he was there."

"Do you get these feelings now, when you're away from him?"

"Once in a while. But it's not an evil feeling like it used to be. Now I appreciate it because it makes me feel like, you know, at least somebody loved me at one time."

"But there was one time when you thought it was an evil feeling?"

"Right."

"Would you be more likely to give in to your father if he was crying or if he was in a rage?"

"If he was in a rage."

"Why would you give in to him when he was in a rage?"

"Because I would be afraid of him. My father is the type of man, when he's in a rage, he's in another world. He would hurt you and feel like shit and want to die later for doing it."

"Did he ever hurt you that way when he wanted sexual relations?"

"No, never."

"Do you think your father ever had relations with your sister?"

"Definitely not."

"Why do you say that?"

"Definitely not, because I know my father."

"What is there about your father that would keep him from having relations with your sister?"

"I don't know how to explain it. I just know him. I probably know him better than any human on earth. And I know that he never would."

"Barbara, I want you to relax now and sleep, relax and sleep before I awaken you. I want you to sleep for ten minutes. Sleep, Barbara, breathe deep and sleep."

Barbara began to twist and turn in her sleep, and I assured her she was all right. I started counting again, but she continued to be agitated. I stopped counting and asked, "What's bothering you?"

She stirred, she retreated as though she were physically attempting to melt into the chair. Then she asked, "Have you ever smelled death?"

"You smell death? Tell me about it."

Barbara began to sob, deep-throated sobs that wracked her whole body. Through the sobs she stammered, "I want to die. I want to die."

"This is very important to you, Barbara, so let me understand your feelings about death. I won't let you be hurt. Relax now, relax."

After a few moments the sobs subsided and she again asked, "Have you ever smelled death?"

"Yes, I have. In the morgue. Have you ever smelled death?"

She hesitated a long time before answering, "I did."

"Tell me about it."

"It was cold. It wasn't cold like feeling—I mean, like air, like weather. It was cold, like chills. It smelled like chloroform. I didn't want to smell it anymore."

"Where were you when you smelled it?"

"I was in the park. The park, and I love the park, and the park, it smelled like death."

"Have you ever met death?"

"I don't think so."

"Has anybody in your family, or anyone close to you, died?"

"No. Nobody's ever died that I know very well."

"Have you ever thought about somebody dying? What it would be like?"

"I thought about myself dying and what other people would think."

"Tell me what they would think."

"They'd be relieved."

"People would be relieved. Who would be relieved if you died?"

"My mother and my father. They'd be relieved."

"Why would your mother be relieved?"

"Then she'd never have to worry about my father leaving her for me."

"This is what death means to you?"

"Yes."

"And how does it make you feel, when you think that your mother would be relieved that you died?"

"I wish that she would understand that my father wouldn't leave her for me. I wouldn't let him. I wish her to feel that way toward me. I wish I could go home to her right now, and just hug her and tell her how much I love her. But I can't." Barbara began to sob again.

"If your mother could believe this, you think that she would love you, don't you? If she could only believe that you loved her and would not steal your father away from her. That's the only thing that keeps her from loving you."

"It is. She's told me that."

"When did she tell you?"

"Lots of times. In a lot of different ways."

"Can you tell me some of the ways?"

"Not always in words. If I sit down next to my father, my mother kind of scrunches in between us. If I get up to get him a cup of coffee, she gets there before I do. And it doesn't mean that she doesn't love me, she just doesn't love me being very close to him. And I can understand that. I really can."

"So, every day, something inside of you says, if only I can convince my mother that I love her and will not take daddy away. That's why you can't say you hate your mother, isn't it?"

"I love my mom. I love her so much." She burst out in tears again.

"You have to reassure her, don't you? You feel so badly about your father loving you, don't you?"

"I used to think it would solve it, if he died, but she'd only be lost. It wouldn't be fair. That's the worst thing that could ever happen."

"Are there times when you wanted him to die?"

"No. I never wanted him to. I thought maybe that would be the solution, but it is no solution. There's nothing there if someone has to die to get it. I love her so much. I need her so much. If she only knew." Barbara was crying freely now. "Why won't my mother love me?"

"Are you sure that's the only reason your mother doesn't love you?"

"I know it is."

"But it's not your fault. It really isn't."

"But it is. There just seems like there's got to be something that I could do. I just can't seem to do it. When I got married, she was so happy. And when we were there for my wedding, it was just beautiful. It was mom and me. For the first time in my life, it was me and mom doing something. She was reassuring me and telling me to calm down. That it was really groovy. And it was what I wanted, so why should I get that upset about it, you know. It was so wonderful."

"Why was she so happy, do you think?"

"Because I had finally found something that I could love and that could love me. And she was so crushed when it—when we broke up."

"Now, Barbara, I want you to listen carefully. If that

was the only thing that kept your mother from loving you, why is it that she could not love the other children?"

"She loved them, but not very much. She wanted daddy for herself completely."

"She had a problem loving any of the children, didn't she?"

"Yeah. Stu she loved very much. Very much."

"Which is sort of the opposite of you and your daddy, isn't it?"

"Uh-huh. But it's not that kind of love."

"No. I realize that."

"But he was the first child and the only one that they really would have accepted. Four was too much. One was just great."

"Was she sort of seductive, though, sometimes around Stu?"

"No! My mother seductive!?"

"Did she get him his coffee?"

"He doesn't drink coffee. She doesn't do anything except fix dinner. And he usually did that himself, too. Stu was a good kid. He's never been in any trouble. Never. Maybe if I'd been halfway decent, I'd have had half a chance. But I wasn't. I was always in trouble."

I made a mental note that she obviously still accepted the blame for her mother's rejection of her as I asked, "What sort of trouble?"

"With the family. Boy, I used to get more spankings. I got more spankings than all the other kids put together."

"Who spanked you?"

"My dad. My mother's never laid a hand on me except that one time when she beat me."

"Your dad would spank you and then love you?"

"Yeah. He'd say, 'Barbie, I'm sorry. God, I'm sorry.' And he'd almost start to cry. But he'd do that any time he had to spank any of us."

I looked at my watch. We had been talking for over an hour and a half. I had tried to discontinue the session some minutes before and I now said, "Barbara,

I want you to relax and sleep for ten minutes. When I awaken you, you'll feel refreshed and you will not recall anything we talked about tonight. You will not recall it until I tell you to. Relax, now breathe deep and sleep."

While she slept, I read through some of the notes I'd made of our prior meetings. Ten minutes later I awakened her and asked how she felt.

She replied, "Marvelous."

Suddenly she frowned. I noticed her reaction.

"What are you thinking?" I asked.

She hesitated a moment before saying, "I don't know why, but I suddenly thought about my dad spanking me. Were we talking about that?"

"As a matter of fact, we were. Do you recall anything else?"

"No. Just something about my dad spanking me."

"Consciously, what do you remember about those spankings?"

"He spanked us a lot, but he hated it. I know his father used to beat him. His father was a—my grandfather is an ex-prizefighter with a terrible temper. And my father was very small. He's only five-eight now and, I understand, when he was twelve, he was about the size of a five- or six-year-old. He's told me that one time my grandfather knocked him through a wall. He gave him a concussion four times. Knocked him out cold six or eight times. My grandfather just had this thing. And so, now, my dad can't stand violence."

"It seems your father suffered a great deal, too."

"Oh, he did. He really did. He had a helluva life. I wouldn't want it. Mine's not half as bad as his was. His was physical violence—physical pain plus mental pain."

"Do you know much about your mother's background?"

"She had the same kind. It was terrible. They both went through hell."

I had tested to see the extent of the emotional impact for the father and mother, but it appeared to be equal, so I returned to the father's early life for more details and said, "Tell me as much as you can about your dad's life."

Barbara relaxed for a few moments, lit a cigarette, and told me that her dad's father died when he was an infant and his mother remarried when he was four. His stepfather moved the family from South Dakota to northern California, but after a short time his mother and stepfather divorced. Without support, he, his mother, brothers, and sisters became transients. Once, on a car trip, Barbara related, her father pointed out the place where he and his family had lived and told her their home had been "four blankets tied between three trees."

Her father's second stepfather, Grandpa Kelly, had been a prizefighter, fisherman, and booze runner—during prohibition—whose favorite hobby was beating up anyone who happened to be around. This included his wife, stepchildren, and everyone at the local pub in what he affectionately referred to as "his donnybrook." "But," Barbara said, "my grandfather Kelly cooled down after he got a little age on him and became a lovable man. He's huge. I mean you can't believe how huge he is. Big fingers, big hands, and now his hands are all knotted up from breaking. He was so strong that when he'd hit somebody, he'd break his knuckles. My father went through hell growing up, and it left quite an impression on him. He doesn't believe in violence at all. He's very peaceable. If he can talk his way out of it, he'd be called a coward before he'd hit anyone."

I asked if her father was a religious person because often a family's religiosity—strict, lax, fundamental, or liberal—can have a direct bearing on the lives of the father, mother, and children. Barbara told me he'd never been religious when he was younger or when he and her mother had married. However, when they moved to Formosa, her dad began teaching four- and five-year-olds in Sunday School and her mother, the six-year-olds.

I asked, "How old were you at that time?"

"Five."

"So your dad became religious about the time you were five."

"Yes, we were all baptized. My father had never been baptized and then all of us, except my mother, were baptized in the Lutheran mission. Then we came to the States, and I don't know if you've ever been to a mission, but it's not like a church. I mean, there were peasants and people—sick people, you know, who were bleeding. They'd all come. It was for everybody and there were no such things as tithes or offerings. I can see that little church as if it was sitting right in front of me now. It was little and white with a bell and you had to go through a rose arbor to get into it. It had like, like a little courtyard—and there was an old woman, she was a nun, but she left the convent and became a Lutheran. My mom and I used to go and have tea with her. She was the caretaker of the place. Her hair was snowy white and she was beautiful with rosy cheeks. And she always wore a little white dress. She was the most fabulous human being. She was just fabulous. I loved her to pieces. She used to let me ring the bell on Sunday afternoon."

"Does your dad pray? I mean, at home, or say grace before dinner?"

"Yeah. He'd say, 'Bless us, oh, Lord, for these, Thy gifts, that we receive from Thy bounty.' We always had to say grace except on Sunday and my mother said it then. We'd each take turns, but I could never say it right. I always got it mixed up. You had to learn grace in Sunday School in Formosa. They'd give us cookies so we'd learn it. But I never got it right even then. I'd always mess it up. We'd have big parades and sing 'Onward, Christian soldiers.' We'd have these parades in the Chinese graveyard above our house. It was about—it seemed like miles, but I guess it was about a half a block above our house."

I wondered if there was a connection between her acid trip and the graveyard in Formosa. "The graveyard was forbidden and you were frightened. Tell me about it."

"The Chinese, at least on Formosa, the wealthy men—well, you see, their servant is usually killed when a wealthy man dies. Or the servant kills himself. Then his head is buried above the ground. It's put on top of the grave so that the servant can look after his master in death as well as he did in life. There were skulls everywhere."

Barbara went on to say that after the skin decomposed and rotted off the skull members of his family would return to dye the jaw bones red and wire them so it looked as though the servant was smiling, showing that he was content to look after his master buried below. She described the funeral procession as being composed not only of family and friends, but of professional mourners who wore gunnysacks over their heads, cried, and threw ashes as everyone walked to the cemetery. Others burned incense below a huge picture they carried of the deceased and a band played as dogs barked and chased the mourners as they marched to the graveyard.

I asked, "What was the climate like in Formosa? Was it damp or dry?"

"It rained just about every day. It was beautiful. It was green. When they'd have typhoons, it'd wash out the bridge and we'd be stuck on that mountain because we lived on the other side on the lower end of Formosa."

"Were there any smells connected with the graveyard?"

"A kind of sickening odor. I can't explain it."

"Musty?"

"It was like death. It was the smell of death."

"You could smell death."

"Yeah. The other kids didn't even seem to notice it, but I did. Maybe they just never said anything. I never said anything, but I could smell it. I could smell death."

There didn't seem to be any connection, at the moment, between Barbara's recollections of a graveyard in

Formosa with those thoughts she had during her acid trip.

"What can you tell me about your mother's background?"

"She was raised by a madman."

"Do you mean that literally?"

"My mother's father was a madman. He was crazy. Absolutely crazy. Today, without a doubt, he would have been committed." When Barbara finished telling me about her grandfather, I was in complete accord.

Her mother was one of seven children—six daughters and one boy. All of the children had been taught from the first years of their lives that they should talk with no one except members of the immediate family. If they were caught speaking to anyone else, they were whipped with a leather strap. Barbara, having seen the strap, described it as triangular, each side about half an inch wide with razor-sharp edges. None of the children were allowed to cut their hair, so when her parents married, her mother's hair was one foot longer than she was tall. Also, her grandfather had a rule that whenever he got up for breakfast, (and that was at 5 A.M.), or came home for dinner, all the children had to be washed, dressed, and seated at the dining room table waiting for him. Barbara's grandmother, never sure at what time he would arrive home from work, would have the children at the table by 4 P.M. They would await his arrival silently, with their hands folded in their laps. At dinner, they had to eat whatever was put on their plate. And even if all they were served was a tablespoon of a vegetable or one small piece of meat, they were not to ask for more. If they did, he would use the whip. Following dinner, they did their homework and chores and went to bed.

I asked, "Did these rules have anything to do with his religious beliefs?"

"No, they were things he dreamt up. He was crazy. I told you, he was absolutely crazy."

"Is he still living?"

"No, he died when my mother was eight or nine. My

grandmother remarried and that man kept trying to fool around with my mother. She told me that one time she had to chase him out of the house with a knife."

Suddenly it was clear why Barbara's mother couldn't face the problems between Barbara and her husband. At this point I terminated our session, said good night to Barbara, and reflected briefly upon her statement that her parents had gone through hell. I had to agree.

After Barbara left, I spent several minutes straightening out my office and locking up. I went to the parking lot, got my car, and was heading home when I saw Barbara standing across the street, thumb in the air, trying to hitch a ride. It had never occurred to me that Barbara did not have transportation and was hitchhiking from Los Angeles to my office in Northridge for our visits. I made a U-turn, stopped, and opened the door. She leaned in, not recognizing me for the moment, and said, "Are you going into Hollywood?"

"I guess I am."

Fifth Visit,

NOVEMBER 19

"Did you ever hear of Amy?" Barbara asked on her next visit to my office.

"Amy? Uh—is that a girlfriend of yours or—" I let the question hang. Barbara laughed uproariously. "Amy isn't a girl. Amy is the grooviest trip in the world." I had more than a working knowledge of most the drugs used by teen-agers, but I had never heard of Amy. "What kind of a drug is it?"

"People use it—I think it's for heart conditions. Something like that. They carry them, break them open, and sniff. It's got a speed-type reaction, but it's like acid, too. It hits you just like—Flash Gordon! The moment you break it open and sniff it, it's in your head and you're stoned. Just like that. Stoned. More stoned than you could imagine you could ever be. Except it only lasts for about three, maybe four minutes."

"Ammonia nitrate?"

"I don't know. It's called amial nitrate, Amy for short."*

Barbara had come in moments before and, after she had settled herself on the couch, I asked if anything

*Amyl: A univalent hydrocarbon radical C_5H_{11}, existing in several isomeric modifications, compounds of which occur in fuel oil, fruit essences, etc.

unusual had occurred since our last meeting. That was when she asked me if I had ever heard of Amy.

"Then it's really like an acid trip, only it lasts a short while?"

"Yeah, but there's, you know, ten or twelve Amys in a box when you buy them. And boy, you get—your head just feels like it's going to burst. You get so stoned! There's a lot of hallucinating, a lot of color. Things happen faster than you can imagine. And if you take a lot of them at one time—I mean, I've been to parties where that's all you took. You come in, you know, 'straight,' and you get a 'head' as you come through the door. And those parties are fabulous. There could be nobody there and you'd still have a wonderful time. It's really groovy. The first time I ever heard of them, I thought, Well, that can't work. Because just sniffing something like that, it's not going to make your head feel great! But it does. It makes your head feel like it's going to break wide open."

"Did you take or sniff an Amy last night?"

"Yeah."

"Alone?"

"Uh-uh, with Sean."

"Who is Sean?"

"A guy."

"Tell me about him."

"He's a guy I met at the bank. He came in one day and I happened to wait on him. Then he'd always come up to me whenever he came into the bank."

"How did you come to see him socially?"

"Well, one day when I was making a deposit for him, he gave me a piece of paper and it had a telephone number on it. I asked, 'Whose number is this?' He said it was his and he hoped I would give him a call when I got off work. I did and he took me out that night."

"What kind of a fellow is he?"

"He's the only guy I know who has things he can brag about and doesn't."

"Compared to whom?"

"Well, like compared to—well, Allan and Ronnie."

"Who are they?"

"A couple of guys."

"Tell me about them."

"I met them at the bank about three weeks ago. They'd come in a couple of times and kind of smiled and looked at me and chatted with me when things weren't too busy. They always came in together and then one day they asked me to go out to lunch with them. I did and we got to be friends. I thought they were the grooviest guys in the world. They were out of sight. Allan offered to buy me a car. And Ronnie offered to get me an apartment for half price."

"How soon after you met them did they offer to do these things for you?"

"At lunch that first day."

"Tell me what they said."

"Allan asked where I lived and when I told him he said that it was pretty far from the bank. Then he asked how I got, you know, went back and forth to work. When I told him by either bus or hitchhiking he said he didn't want me hitchhiking anymore and he would see what he could do about getting me a car. I thought he was putting me on and I said something like, 'Oh, sure! Just like that you're going to give me a car.' But he explained that he wasn't going to give me a car, just make the down-payment, and although I'd have to keep up the monthlies, I wouldn't have to pay back the money he laid out. I said, 'Groovy, if you mean it,' and he said, 'I do.' Then Ronnie said, 'I'm not sure, but I think I can get you an apartment for half price. I'll check on it and let you know.' Well, he called me at the bank the next day and said that his friend owned some apartment buildings and he owed Ronnie a lot of favors. Anyway, Ronnie's friend agreed to give me an apartment for seventy-five a month in this really groovy building. That's what I mean, they were really groovy guys. But Sean offers absolutely nothing but his companionship, and yet, I feel very close to him. I could—I wouldn't mind going to bed with Sean. I might even enjoy it."

"Do you often have these feelings toward men?"

"No. That's what's so strange about it."

"But you have gone to bed with men before. Do you go to bed without these feelings?"

"Uh-huh. I'm a very lonely person. Anything to seem like someone cares for me is welcome. But then, afterward, you know it's not that at all."

I made a mental note to explore Barbara's relationships with Sean, Allan, and Ronnie when she was under hypnosis and switched topics by asking, "Do you still miss your husband?"

"A little. Especially when I'm alone."

"Barbara, it's almost three weeks since our first meeting and I wondered if you've thought any more about the real reason behind your marriage breaking up. Do you have a better idea of what caused it now?"

"Yeah, I've thought about it. And I guess it was when Bob realized I wasn't lying about the problem with my dad. I don't know why he suddenly realized it, but he did. I don't know if I told you that he went to a psychiatrist and the psychiatrist told Bob it was true—that these things happen. I guess it scared him."

"In what way did it scare him?"

"Well, like, sometimes—I used to see my father when I was with Bob, you know, in bed. And sometimes I would call him dad—things like that."

"Did Bob ever meet your dad?"

"Oh, sure—Bob adored him. If you met my father, you couldn't help but like him. He's the most fantastic man. He really is."

"Did Bob meet him before or after you told him about your relationship?"

"Afterward."

"And he adored him?"

Barbara nodded, "Bob went up there intending to smack him on the nose. But after he met my dad, he couldn't. You just can't get mad at my dad. It makes it even hard to believe that what's happened has happened. He's the most—actually, he's the most fantastic man I know. Really. He really is. He's got more going for him than anyone else I've ever met."

"In what way?"

"He has a wonderful personality. He can talk to anybody on any subject. I've never heard him stumped for words, never. He can do almost anything and do it very, very well. I don't know anything he can't do. He's just a fantastic man. And he's willing to do or try anything."

"How did Bob get along with your mother?"

"Groovy. He thought she was fantastic, too. She's the kind of person, you know, that's kind of in the background. You didn't really notice her, but when you think back on it, she made the situation what it was. She's a wonderful cook. She may not be the kind of hostess that women are here in L. A., but she makes everybody feel very at home."

"I was under the impression that you felt she was never the mother that you wanted or needed."

"Right! I just wish she could have been all she was, plus a lady. To look like a lady and not a motorcycle rider. Everybody else thinks this is groovy. You know, 'Wow, that's your mom on a motorcycle! Out of sight!' But, if she's your mom, you want her to be a mom. You want her to be around all the time, not just when people are there. I demand a lot from people and if they don't measure up, I put them 'down' in my book. I see their good points, but I wish they had more. My mom is a wonderful person. She's very intelligent. She's a lifetime member of the Beta Club and a straight-A student."

I told Barbara to hold on for a moment while I changed the tape on the casette recorder. While I was changing the tape, Barbara began to giggle. When the tape was in place and turned back on, I asked, "What's so funny?"

"I was thinking about last night and Sean," Barbara said.

"Tell me about it."

"Well, we were laying there, dressed, and he kissed me. Then we sat up and Bob Dylan was on the stereo and Sean said, 'Get it, Dylan, get it,' then to me, 'You know, I had you undressed and in bed already. We're gonna have to cool it.' Which I thought was absolutely dumb."

"So you got in bed and he told you to cool it?"

"Yeah, he said we'd have to cool it. So we watched television with the sound off and the stereo turned on. It was really groovy—out of sight."

"Were you stoned?"

"Not really—like I said before, on Amys. When I get home tonight, I'm going to call Sean. He'll probably be in bed because he's got to work tomorrow morning—he's a hairdresser. He only has to work three days a week to make enough money to live on. That tears me up! Someday I'm going to have everything. I'm going to have the whole world at my feet!"

"Does Sean know the other two men you mentioned, Allan and Ronnie?"

"No."

"By the way, did you take the offer of the apartment or the car that Allan and Ronnie made?"

"No, and I'm not going to. I'm not going to see those guys anymore. They hang me up. They put me on a bummer."

"Tell me about it."

"They're so much in love with themselves. So much concerned with their own lives. Sean made me see this. Because, you know, he wanted to know about *me*. He asked how *my* day was. What *I* liked? Not, *I* want to do this. Or, *I'm* going to do this tomorrow. He asked, 'What are *you* doing tomorrow?' It was groovy. It makes a big difference. I mean, he would ask me and he wanted to know. We've talked about horses and all sorts of groovy things. It had nothing to do with sex. Just that one statement, which was so hilarious."

"Was sex part of the offer that Allan and Ronnie made to you regarding the apartment and car?"

"Not in the beginning. They told me they both had

girlfriends and they weren't interested in me sexually. But I found out that wasn't true. I mean, they didn't come right out and say that if we didn't have sex there was no car and apartment. But that's what it really came down to. They figured they could talk me into it. It seems that what they had in mind was dual control. The two of them and me."

"You mean at the same time or on different nights?"

"Together."

"They told you that?"

"They were very honest about it. Allan said, 'We both think you're very groovy and we want to have you together.' I said, 'You want to do what?!' I couldn't believe it."

"And it hadn't occurred to you that there was sex connected with their offer?"

"It did, but they convinced me I was wrong. And I thought, 'Wow! Out of sight! I've got something good going here.' I thought everything was really groovy. And then—Flash Gordon! Suddenly it wasn't."

"Why do you think two total strangers would offer you a car and an apartment at half price?"

"People have done things like that for me before."

"No strings attached?"

"No strings attached. Guys are like that when they're young and have money. They want to spend it on somebody. And they want to spend it on you."

"Who's done that with you?"

"When I first moved down to L. A. The people I lived with panhandled for me every day. I mean, it was seven to ten dollars a night and they'd give it all to me. And all I'd do was sit around and do absolutely nothing. There were other girls in the house. They all had to work but I never had to do a thing. Nobody expected anything of me. They gave me food, they gave me whatever I wanted plus the money that they panhandled."

"Were these diggers, or what?"

"No, it was just a house full of people. They weren't really diggers. They weren't that grubby. They weren't that down. These people all had money except for the girls that lived there. And the girls that lived there—the guys'd put them on bummers because I never had to do a thing. They didn't ask me to clean the house or anything. I usually cooked dinner because the two girls were terrible cooks. But I didn't have to do it. I did it because I wanted to. The guys couldn't have cared less."

"How old were they?"

"The girls were, I don't know—eighteen, maybe twenty. Around that age. The guys, twenty-one to twenty-three. Some in their late twenties."

"How many were there?"

"Three girls besides me, and five guys. The guys'd take me out to clubs; they'd take me anywhere I wanted to go and never ask anything of me. And the girls—you know, they made them leave, but then, more girls moved in. They made the other girls leave because the girls didn't want to clean the house. I didn't do anything. I didn't clean the house. But they didn't make me leave."

"Did the guys work?"

"Uh-huh. Everyone worked, except the girls. One of the guys worked at Blue Cross and the rest were musicians or managers. You know, managers for musicians. They all made pretty good money and they all had beautiful, beautiful cars. Sports cars and stuff."

"Then why were they out begging for money?"

"Oh, the guys didn't. Just the girls. And they begged for money for me. Think of that, they were out there working for me. I tried panhandling one night, and I just couldn't do it."

"I was under the impression that you had panhandled for money."

"No, I tried it one time. I made money selling the *Free Press*—but that's not panhandling."

"How did the guys feel when you didn't want to panhandle to bring in money?"

"They'd say, 'Well, you're too intelligent, Barbara. You've got more on the ball than to do something like that. It's beneath you to do that kind of stuff and we don't really want you doing it.' Obviously it made me feel good. Like I was something special after all."

"How did the entire relationship make you feel?"

"It was strange. That's why I moved. Too much was being done for me and I was losing my independence. I didn't want that."

I was reasonably certain that her interpretation of the motivations of the others was fantasy. The situations were undoubtedly true but her interpretations were not. Her perception of the events was simply a projection of her intense need to be smothered with love and completely indulged. Her statement regarding her fear of losing her independence was merely another form of self-delusion. Barbara was an extremely dependent person. Her dependency needs were not met because she depended on the type of people who were as irresponsible as she. She was not afraid of dependency—she was afraid of responsibility. However, Barbara was not ready to accept this interpretation and I was forced to continue as though I believed her account.

"They weakened you by giving you too much." Barbara nodded as I continued, "As a matter of fact, this has been sort of a crippling thing all of your life, hasn't it?"

"Yes. Every time I get ahold of something good, it turns into shit. It always has."

"Why do you say that?"

"Look at my whole life. When I think back, my greedy half looks at it and says, 'If you'd kept your mouth shut, then look at what you would have had, materially.' I'd have had a car, I'd have had anything I wanted! Then I look at it from my other half, from the good part of me, and I'd say, 'Look at how many people you've messed up. If you'd never been born, it never would have happened. All the pain could have been averted. All those people would never have been hurt. And your mother and father would have lived happily ever after.' All of these things come to my mind. Every job that I've ever gotten that was really, really worth having I've blown through my own stupidity. I blew the job of a parts manager in a very large automotive supply house up in Farrell. I've always messed up my chances of having friends. Especially girlfriends because I would end up with their boyfriends, and, you know, it's like a catastrophe for one girl to take another girl's boyfriend. And even though I never, never intended to, I'd usually end up with their guys. Like with Rozelle. They'd tell her to cool it. They'd say, 'I don't like you any more. I like Barbara.' I guess that's why Rozelle is so against me. Because from the first time we met, we had this competitive thing."

"Had you taken any of her boyfriends?"

"Every one she ever had." Barbara laughed at the thought and through her laughter she continued, "That's no kidding. And I never wanted them. I'd just start talking to them, and they'd say, 'Why can't Rozelle ever talk like that? You know, just talk.' "

"You said that you had messed up your parents' lives, and yet you've given the impression that your parents are fairly happy."

"They are, but now they're afraid of me. Can you imagine having your parents afraid of you? That you might go to the authorities to get what you want? They know how greedy I am. They're afraid that I would do just that."

I studied Barbara for a moment, making sure her attention was completely on me before saying, "Actually, there are two parts of you. One is a greedy manipulating type of person."

Barbara nodded, "Very calculating, very cold."

"And who really—I don't know whether you do it consciously or whether it's just a habit, but you really know how to manipulate people—to get what you want from them."

"I think it's a habit. Because when I think about it later, I feel like shit for doing it. Then I usually try to right my wrong which usually messes it up even worse."

"Perhaps you're trying to punish yourself in some way by messing things up."

Barbara stared at me and after a moment said, "I'll have to think about that."

I returned to our previous conversation and said, "When you were living at the house with the others, the girls who panhandled and worked for you, were you cold and calculating and manipulating them?"

"I guess so, but it wasn't intentional."

"Did you ever have sexual relations with any of the men there?"

"Yes."

"With how many of them?"

"Just with Mark, the owner of the house. He cared a great deal about me. He probably would have married me, had I stayed. I'm sure he would've. But I didn't want to get married. It was enough for me that someone cared. And he did care."

"How old was he?"

"Twenty-seven."

"How old were you at that time?"

"Seventeen."

"Barbara, I'm going to put you to sleep now. I want you to relax. I'm going to turn the lights off so that the design will flash and you'll fall into a deep, sound sleep. A very deep, a very sound sleep." I began to count and Barbara fell into a rhythmic breathing and in moments she was asleep. As I put her into a deeper sleep, she suddenly began to cry. I tried to relax her but was unable to. I asked what was troubling her.

"The Christmas decorations on Hollywood Boulevard."

I was curious and asked why the Christmas decorations upset her. She replied, "Because Christmas isn't going to be anything for me this year. I don't even want it to come. I've got nobody, and Christmas is a time of love and people caring about you and the people you care about. I haven't got anybody that I want to buy a gift for." Then, through her sobs, she continued, "My birthday is the next day. My birthday is the next day and I don't have anybody. I don't have anybody who loves me. Nobody. I want somebody to say, 'Here, Barbara, this is for you.' "

"You want people to give you gifts?"

"And I want to be able to say, 'Thanks, and here's one for you. Have a merry Christmas.' But there isn't anybody. Not anybody." There was a burst of deep sobbing, and when it subsided, and almost as if she were in a dream, she went on, "I wish I was home and everybody was starting to plan for Christmas. We'd talk about what we were going to get each other and us kids'd figure out how to get mom and dad something really nice. But I have nothing now. Nobody. I can't even wonder what anybody is going to get me because there isn't anybody."

"There isn't anybody to give you anything."

"Not with love. I want somebody to give me something because they care about me. And the gift would be a show of caring, but there isn't anybody. There just isn't anybody!" Then, in an anguished scream, "I wish Christmas wouldn't come this year! Dr. Woodbury! Dr. Woodbury! Can you please stop Christmas from coming?"

It took several minutes before Barbara's cries subsided sufficiently for me to attempt to assure her that everything would be all right. That somehow her Christmas was going to be a happy one. At that moment I wasn't quite sure how I could make her Christmas a happy one, but I felt that she needed the assurance.

I questioned Barbara at some length about her finances and learned that she earned between forty and fifty dollars a week as a part-time employee at the bank. She paid twenty-seven dollars a week for rent and the only night she was sure of eating dinner was on Friday, right after she'd been paid. Truthfully, I had not given much thought to Barbara's finances after we had agreed upon a reduced fee for her visits. She had, at that time, stated that she could not afford my normal charges, but I had not realized that even the agreed sum was a hardship. I made a mental note to discontinue any further charges. During the questioning I learned, too, that her husband, Bob, had not left her any money when he instituted suit for the annulment. Nor did she have money to meet any emergency that might arise. She lived, literally, from day to day. The few dollars she earned selling the *Free Press* on Sunset Boulevard in Hollywood was the only "luxury money" she had.

Both Barbara and I needed relief from the intense emotion that had built up between and within us, and I let her rest for ten minutes. I used the time for relaxation, too, and then initiated a new direction by utilizing what I call "hypnotic free association." I told Barbara to let her mind drift, that I wanted her to dream. I wanted her to dream about anything at all. After a few moments I asked what she was dreaming about and she replied, "Marianne."

"Tell me about Marianne."

"She's a little girl in Formosa. I told her my secret."

"You did tell your secret then?"

"Uh-huh, that's the only time."

"How old are you?"

"Seven."

"And what did you say to her?"

Barbara regressed to the high-pitched voice of a little girl and said, "I have a secret. And she said, 'Tell me what it is.' And I said, 'No. It's between my daddy and me. It's our secret, and you can't know.' And Marianne said, 'I'll tell you a secret, if you tell me your secret.' And I said, 'Okay, what's your secret?' And she said, 'My brother and I take a bath together.' That's what Marianne told me. And I had to tell her my secret because I promised. I said, 'My daddy and I play a game.' And she wanted to know how to play it. And I told her there wasn't much to it. And she said she

A CASE HISTORY OF INCEST

wanted to learn how. She wanted to know what kind of game it was. So I went home and told my daddy, and he seemed very upset at first, but then he said, 'Okay.' He wanted to play too. So Marianne came over, and we played the game. It made me mad."

"Why did it make you mad?"

"Because daddy played it with Marianne. And it was *our* game."

"Barbara, I want you to go back, I want you to go back in time and relive those moments. I want you to tell me the conversation that took place."

Barbara stirred, the muscles on her face moved, and she wrinkled her nose and frowned. She gasped and said, "I don't want to."

"Why don't you want to tell me?"

"I don't like Marianne."

"You're angry with her. Is that the only reason you don't want to tell me?"

"Daddy said I'm not supposed to talk about it. Not to tell anybody."

I realized I had made a mistake. I had said, *"Barbara, I want you. . . ."* I said quickly, "Do you think Cindy might tell me?" Barbara giggled. I continued, "You like Cindy don't you?"

"Yeah, but she's a blabbermouth," Barbara answered.

"That's one of the reasons I like her," I countered.

Barbara didn't say anthing for a few moments and then, in her little-girl voice, began, "We had a long hall. Daddy's bedroom was at the end of the hall, mine was next and then Stu's and Holly's. Then there was the living room and the kitchen on the other side of the bathroom, and there was a dining room. We walked in and Marianne said, 'Where's your daddy?' And I said, 'He's in the bedroom.' And she said, 'Where do you play the game?' And I said, 'In the bedroom.' She was kind of scared because I didn't tell her what kind of a game it was, only that it was fun and that it tickled. But she wanted to know so we went down there and she said, 'First, you and your daddy show me how to play.' And I said, 'Okay." And daddy said, 'Okay,' too. And he told Marianne, 'You mustn't tell anybody because the game that we're going to play is a secret and we can't let anybody know our secret. Okay?' And Marianne said, 'Okay, I won't tell anybody.' She even crisscrossed and hoped to die. So daddy and I played the game and then daddy played the game with Marianne. Only she laughed. I didn't laugh but she did. And that made me mad because I didn't think she would laugh. But she did.

"When Cindy and Marianne walked into the bedroom, did her father ask both of them to get undressed?"

"Uh-uh," Barbara said as she shook her head. "He undressed us. He always undressed Cindy. And he undressed Marianne. She giggled a lot."

"Do you think she knew what was going on?"

"I don't think so. I don't know."

"What happened then?"

"Then Marianne and I went back to her. . . ." Barbara suddenly shuddered and squirmed in her chair and I asked, "What's the matter?"

"Nothing," Barbara almost whispered.

"Something bothers you. Something bothered Cindy." Barbara refused to speak for several moments. I said nothing and I waited as she continued to squirm. Finally she mumbled, "Cindy and Marianne got under Marianne's bed and played the game."

"Why does that bother Cindy?"

"Because Cindy's grown-up and she knows right from wrong."

"What do you mean?"

"Cindy can think back and realize how wrong it was."

"Why do you say it was wrong?"

"Because Cindy and Marianne are both girls. It's wrong. It's wrong!"

"You feel it's wrong."

"Yes!" Barbara cried out, almost shouting her answer.

A CASE HISTORY OF INCEST 109

I watched her for a moment and said, "You're undergoing an emotion now. Tell me what it is."

"Disgust. I don't want to talk about it. It's ugly. I don't want to think about it anymore."

"All right. Push it away if you want to. But I'm going to tell you something, and you have to trust me and believe me. All little boys and all little girls sometimes play the game with one another."

"That's wrong. It's very wrong."

Again, using the technique of speaking to the unconscious, I said, "Children, particularly at that age, are innocent. Now, the thing that makes it wrong is the knowledge. In the Bible, there's a story about Adam and Eve. I'm sure you know the story. They took some fruit from the Tree of Knowledge. It was the knowledge that made them feel bad—to feel guilty. They were innocent until they took the knowledge. Do you understand?"

"I think so," she mumbled.

"And you were innocent until you had the knowledge."

"But the picture haunts me."

"Do you dream about it?"

"Yes. Not often. But I dream about it. And after I do, I can't sleep. I don't know why it bothers me so much, but it does."

"Because you do not know how to accept yourself."

"I get chills just thinking about it."

"Did anything further occur because of your telling Marianne the secret?"

"She told her father."

"Ahh! And what happened?"

"He didn't believe it."

"He didn't believe it?"

"No. Daddy told me later, not to ever, ever tell the secret again."

"Would you have felt better if Marianne's father had talked to your dad?"

"No! No! No! He and dad were good friends. And I

didn't want to break up their friendship. And it would have, if he had believed it."

"So as far as you know, no adult has ever known about your father's behavior?"

"My mother knew. She didn't know then. She didn't know until much later."

"I mean, at any time, have any other adults suspected your relationship with your dad?"

"Yeah. My dad's best friend, Brian Reynolds."

"Tell me about that."

"And his other best friend, Jack Sanders. They asked me about it. About a year ago. To Brian I confessed. To Jack I didn't. I confessed to Brian because Brian could be a help to dad. Dad doesn't know that any of his friends know. It would crush him. He wouldn't ever be able to face them again."

"Do you know what made them suspect?"

"It was the unnatural closeness my dad and I had. It was obvious. No father takes his daughter to places he doesn't take his wife. No father takes his daughter when he could be taking his wife. No father spends all of his waking hours talking to his daughter. Any time that either of them would come over, I was with dad."

"Almost a boyfriend-girlfriend relationship?"

"Almost, yeah. He would walk with his arm around me and things like that. And you know, my dad doesn't look that old. He looks very, very young. It made me feel dumb though. I mean, it's like having your grandmother holding your hand when you walk across the street. It's stupid, and it embarrassed me."

"Why did you let him do it?"

"Because he needed me."

"He needed you?"

"Yes."

"Do you think they've ever discussed this matter with your dad?"

"I'm sure they haven't. I would have known about it. Boy! Would I have known about it."

I continued to question Barbara about her relationship with Marianne but it seemed to revolve around the one isolated incident. When I felt I had exhausted the questioning for the night, I said, "I'm going to awaken you soon, Barbara. Is there anything you want to tell me before I do?"

"I think I might be pregnant."

Just like that, easily, without any inflection or raising of her voice, once again showing the typical lack of emotion of the psychopath, Barbara told me this news. "Do you know who the father is?"

"Cory."

"Cory? Have you told me about him?"

"I don't know. I don't think so. I'm not sure if I'm pregnant. I had my period when he balled me. I don't know if you can get pregnant then or not."

"Have you been to bed with anyone else recently?"

"Nope. Only Cory. You see, I stopped taking birth control pills and that sometimes messes up my period. So I might just be messed up."

"Are you worried about it?"

"Uh-huh."

"Does Cory know about it?"

"Nope. And he's not going to know. Even if I am. I'm going to find someone to give me an abortion. Could you help me get an abortion?"

"We'll see about it. If you are pregnant, there are legal means to obtain abortions."

After getting the answer I did the last time I had asked if there was anything she wanted to tell me, I was a little apprehensive about asking the question again, but I did. When she assured me there was nothing more on her mind at that moment, I put her into a deeper sleep, told her to relax, and then awakened her. As I awakened her, I again emphasized that she would not be able to recall anything that we had talked about, that I would let her remember at the proper time. I scheduled another appointment with her for the following week; however, it didn't work out that way as I was to learn four days later when I received a phone call.

An Interview with Paul,

NOVEMBER 25

"Dr. Woodbury?"
"Yes."
"My name is Paul Jackson. I'm a friend of Barbara's."

Paul went on to tell me that Barbara had asked him to call to let me know that she had been very ill—a strep throat—and that her parents had driven down to take her home. I asked how long he had known Barbara and learned they'd been good friends for about a month. I thought an interview with Paul might be helpful in giving me another view of Barbara—a view of her by one of her peers. Paul was reluctant to see me but he finally acquiesced.

We met two days later in Hollywood. Paul was a nice-looking boy, about nineteen, with flashing, blue eyes. He had thick, tousled brown hair, and a very definite New England accent. Although dressed like a hippie, he seemed motivated to find a job. He had come to Los Angeles about six weeks prior to meeting Barbara and had been working in a coffee shop on Hollywood Boulevard until a short time before. He had completed high school, had no desire to go to college, and had come to California to look around. For what? He wasn't sure. He was extremely reluctant to let me

A CASE HISTORY OF INCEST 113

tape the interview and it took me over thirty minutes to persuade him to agree.

As he had stated on the phone, he had met Barbara the first time about a month ago and they had met the second time the previous week walking on Hollywood Boulevard. He told me, "We were fooling around. Like she told me she was hungry. So I bought her some spaghetti. Shit, we were laughing and I told her she was sucking me in."

"What do you mean, she was sucking you in?"

"You know, taking me for my money. And I didn't have any. I told her, 'You chicks are all alike.' You know, I was playing with her head."

"What happened then?"

"Well, you know, we got to fooling around, and walking around, and—we went up to her place. She let me spend the night there."

"Did you have sexual relations?"

Paul reacted to the question, almost startled. He turned toward me and said, "That ain't none of your fucking business."

Paul was definitely wary of talking to me about their relationship in spite of my showing him my credentials and several minutes were spent convincing him that any information he might be able to give me might be helpful to Barbara. I asked again, "Did you have any physical relationship, sexual relationship, with Barbara?"

"No. No scene like that. But, I think maybe I could have."

"But you didn't?"

"No, but we got along real good. I remember—'cause like—we were laying there on the bed, man, and looking out the window. We were stoned on our ass. We were just laughing and laughing all night long. I had a couple of joints and we were really stoned on our ass, man."

"Would it embarrass you to tell me if you had relations with her?"

"Well, I still don't know too much about you, you know."

"What did she tell you about her dad?"

"That was terrible."

"Well, because of that relationship, Barbara has several hang-ups. One is, she doesn't enjoy sex."

"That's a lie, man. She dug it when we balled. She really dug it. She told me she dug it. In fact, we were going to live together."

"Then you did have sexual relations with her."

"Yeah, man. We did."

"Did she have an orgasm?"

"A what?"

"A climax?"

"A climax—what the hell is that?"

"Did she come?"

"Why didn't you say that in the first place, man?" Before I could reply he went on, "I think she did, really. More than once, maybe. I balled her more than once. And I know what I'm doing, more than she did."

"Was she aggressive in her lovemaking?"

"No. Well, she was pretty aggressive, I guess. I mean, like she was happy, man. That's all I know. I don't know how to say it."

"How long were you with her?"

"Oh, like the last five days. See, like one day we took my laundry out, my rent was due, I wasn't living anyplace then and I didn't have any bread, so I had to move out of my pad and she let me stay with her."

"Were you in the apartment when her parents came down to pick her up?"

"Yeah. Yeah. She was really sick, man. I even had to put her junk together for her."

"Did they know you had been staying at her place with her?"

"I don't think so, but you know—some of my stuff was there. My suitcase was in the room, unpacked, and she told them that she was going to give me the room since her rent was paid till the end of the week. And, uh—they bought it."

"What was your impression of her parents?"

"Her mom was wearing slacks and—she looked, you know, neat—no makeup or nothing, but she looked okay."

"What about her dad?"

"Her dad is a creep."

"A creep?"

"Yeah, a creep."

"Would you describe him to me?"

"Well, he's not too big. And I'd like to punch him in the mouth. And you can tell him I said so."

"Why?"

"I didn't say nothing to him at all and you know what he does? He starts bragging about all the broads he has balled. He's a creep, a goddamn creep."

"Did he ask about your relationship with Barbara?"

"No, nothing like that. She told him, you know, that I was really great. You know, that I helped her, that I'd gone out at night to get her soup and shit like that. I think that's how I got my cold."

Other than that Paul hadn't had too much conversation with Barbara's parents. He helped them down with her baggage and they left by car for Farrell.

I tried to learn as much about Barbara as I could from Paul and asked if he knew Sean, Allan, or Ronnie. He didn't know any of them but he did know Cory. I asked if he thought Cory had had sexual relations with Barbara and he was adamant. He said, "No way. No way at all." I asked how he could be so positive, and he said, "Because Barbara told me. I had said to her that she must have had a good time in bed with him. And she got up-tight. She asked me how I could even think of that."

I asked what he thought of Cory and he said, "He's about the wildest asshole I've ever met. The poor kid is sick. He's an acid head."

"He's dropped acid?"

"Yeah, man. Somebody turned him onto a trip. And you know, you have to have a certain amount of brains —not just any asshole can drop acid. Acid is strong stuff. It can mess you up. Especially if you're not stable. That clown—he's scrambled enough to jump out a window."

"Paul, how long did you know Barbara before she told you about her father?"

"The first night over at my pad. I had no place to go or nothing to do. I wasn't working, you know, and I was really mad at myself because I wasn't working. You have to work or else you're not going to make it. So we were at my house and she asked me to thumb up to Farrell with her to see her mother for Thanksgiving. She said she wanted to say hi, that she missed her mother and her kid sister because they were very close. The three of us were up in my room. Cory was the other one. And Cory kept saying he wanted to go, but Barbara said she didn't want to go unless I did. Then, I don't know what happened, but she told Cory to leave. She got real pissed off at him. She told him to go screw and all that shit—that she never wanted to see him again. She really blew her top. I told her she was being pretty hard on the guy, I mean—put yourself in his place. I didn't dig Cory too much, but still, you know, he was full of shit and all that, but what the hell. Anyway, I was going to leave, just go out because I couldn't stand being with that cat, Cory. And Barbara says, 'Paul, please don't leave. All the things we talked about, it's like I've known you for twenty years. Don't you care for me, at all?' And she went on with that kind of shit, and I told her, 'Yeah, I do care for you. But Cory is a clown and I can't stand him.' I guess I was stoned, or something, and I couldn't put up with him. Yeah, I *was* stoned. And I had turned Cory on to a joint. Anyway, Cory finally beat his ass out of there and then Barbara kept pleading with me, hugging and kissing me and all that shit. Then we lit up a couple more joints and we really got stoned. Then, after a while, we got dressed, and we started to go thumbing— you know, up to Farrell, and then I began thinking about it. It was over four hundred goddamned miles. And I thought, 'Who is this chick that I don't know for shit.' I mean, I know she wouldn't put the boot to me or screw me, but still, goddamnit, four hundred miles. Eight hundred miles round trip, you know? And I just couldn't do it. I told her to forget it and she started to cry. I told her I was sorry, I just couldn't go. I felt real bad about it. I had nowhere to go. But, still, I didn't want to go way up there. I told her I'd get some bread so she could go home. Take a bus or a plane or some goddamned thing—you know, and get up there. Then she said, 'I can't go home. I can't go because of my father.' And I said, 'Why not?' And she said, 'Have you ever heard of....' What's that thing called?"

"Incest?"

"Yeah, incest. And I asked her what that was. And when she told me, I couldn't believe it. I thought it was something that animals did. And there she was, goddamnit, she's telling me that her father and her—I think she said something like from the time she was two or three and I said, 'Don't tell me that shit.' I mean, man, I was really torn up inside. I thought she was kidding me. I just couldn't believe that that fucking asshole had been banging her since she was two."

"Did she tell you that he had intercourse with her?"

"I don't remember. I remember in the back of my mind I kept saying, 'Oh, God, I hope not!' Was he really banging her?" Paul asked, an anxious look on his face.

"I don't think so."

"Well, if he wasn't banging her, what could he have...." Paul broke off, then startled by his own realization, "Do you mean he was going down on her?" Before I could affirm or deny his thought, Paul said, "Oh, no! Don't tell me that! Please I don't even want to talk about that shit."

"Paul, unfortunately those things exist."

"Oh, my! What a fucking world! You mean he really did that to a two- or three-year-old kid?"

"These things do happen."

"And what was she doing while he...." Again Paul broke off, frightened by his own thoughts. After a moment he forced himself to ask, "Do you mean that she was blowing him?!" Before I could say anything, Paul went on, "Don't tell me that! Oh, shit! No! Don't tell me that!" Then, after a long moment, he added, "But you know, after meeting him, I believe it. He's a fucking creep. A goddamn fucking creep."

"Now, in your relationship with Barbara did you engage in any other sexual practice—other than intercourse?"

"Oh, shit, man! I wish I knew you better."

"I am here, Paul, to help Barbara. That's the only interest I have. I am not personally concerned or curious about your sex life."

"Well, I guess—you're sure I'll be helping her?"

"Anything I can learn from you regarding Barbara will be helpful."

"Okay, yeah—she blew me."

"Did you do anything to encourage her to blow you?"

"Shit, man, I don't know how it happened. I mean, we were pretty fucking stoned. Well, like hell man, I didn't force it—goddamn it."

"Did you engage in a similar practice on Barbara?"

"No. I mean—I make that scene, but I didn't feel it with her."

"Now, at any time while you were with her, did you discuss with her the fact that she might become pregnant?"

"I don't know—she said to me, man, I remember, like we were laying in bed one day and she said, 'What happens if I become pregnant?' You know, I had been fooling around and I said, 'Do you have any money? If you have money, I'll marry you.' I was playing with her head again, you know."

"Is that the only time it was mentioned?"

"No. Shit, man—for a while she kept talking about it all the time. Like maybe she wanted to become pregnant. Like she kept saying, 'Paul, what happens if I become pregnant?' You know, at one time, I think she liked me a lot."

"Did she say anything, before leaving, about how long she expected to be away or when she might be back?"

"She said she'd be back someday."

"How did you feel when she left?"

"After I saw her drive away with that savage, you know, that beast—I went back up to the room and, I hate to admit it, but I cried—I really did, man. I cried about her."

After four days had passed and I hadn't heard from Barbara, I had my secretary call her parents' home in Farrell. She talked to Barbara and learned that she was feeling much better and would get in touch with me when she returned to L. A.

Sixth Visit,

DECEMBER 9

Two weeks later I had a collect call from Farrell. Barbara informed me that she would be back in Los Angeles the following day and she said she would like to see me in the evening.

When she came in, she looked paler than when I had last seen her and she also looked as though she had lost weight, but her eyes were as bright and shining as ever. After the usual amenities we settled down to business and I asked her how things had gone at home.

She said, "I couldn't believe it. Nothing has changed—all the same shit. My very first day at home, you know, the morning after we got back there, my dad said to me, 'You shouldn't have come back,' and here I was, you know, really sick. I had a hundred and three temperature and I couldn't hardly talk and would you believe it, here I am laying there and he makes a pass at me. I told him it was ridiculous. And he said I should not have come home. I told him I didn't come home, that he came down and got me—and wouldn't you know it, he makes another pass at me. When I left home yesterday, you know what he said? He told me, 'I'm glad you're leaving because I couldn't keep my hands off you for another day.' He really gave me a bad time. Every other word, whether people were there or not. They didn't understand the meaning behind what he

A CASE HISTORY OF INCEST 121

said, you know—but I did. It was really a bad scene."

"How did your mother react to it?"

"She acted like nothing was going on. She kind of shut it out. Like it was nothing."

"Since your mother was aware of the problem between you and your father, shouldn't you have confronted him with it in her presence?"

"I thought of it. But I can't see any point in crushing her anymore. I feel that it's his problem now. She'd done her bit. She really has. Short of divorcing him, which would be ridiculous because of the people involved, she really has done everything she can."

Barbara was still unable to express the hostility she felt toward her mother. Recovery could not be accomplished until she gained insight into these feelings.

I asked her to tell me everything she could remember from the time her parents arrived in Los Angeles to pick her up until her return earlier in the day. She said that her parents seemed very concerned about her when they arrived, but while packing for her they began to "bitch and moan" about all the things she had accumulated. And they continued to "piss and moan" about them all the way home. Also, they were particularly upset about Bob and insisted it was Barbara's fault that he had all the wedding gifts. They felt that she should have them, and, furthermore, they blamed her for the breakup of her marriage. When they arrived home they had her sleep on the living room sofa because her strep throat was contagious and they didn't want the other children exposed to it. She also overheard them telling the other children that they planned to get her out as soon as possible—that she was intruding. And they blamed her because they had caught Holly, her younger sister, smoking marijuana.

I asked Barbara if she'd been aware that Holly was on pot.

"No. Absolutely not. If I had known, I would have broken her neck. I don't feel that she is mature enough to decide whether she should smoke pot or not. I told Holly, 'It's your life—screw it up. I don't care.' But,

John, I do care and it tears me apart. It was just a mud-slinging week, all of it. I couldn't wait to leave. It was terrible. I never realized how much I appreciated my tenement room and having no money. Having nothing. Having nothing to eat. It was a lot better than being home. I don't think I'll ever go back."

"You will eventually."

"I'm not going to go back and listen to that. I only went back because they came and got me. I thought, Wow! They care. They're coming to get me and they really want me. But they didn't. All they did was bitch about having to drive four hundred miles to pick me up. Then they said that Paul was living with me. And that I was really 'out on the streets,' all kinds of shit. It was really bad. But I had good times with my brothers. And all my old boyfriends came over, and they were so happy to see me, the whole bit."

"By the way, until Paul called me, you had never mentioned him," I offered.

"Well, you see, after I had seen you that last time—whenever that was, I—well, John, I quit my job. I didn't tell you, but...."

"Go on."

"Anyway, I met Paul that night. The night I quit my job. I think it was a week before Thanksgiving. And the night I met him he got kicked out of his room. I think that was on a Thursday, and the next day we were going to hitchhike up to see my folks. We went to his place and started to move his stuff out to my room but that's when I got sick. And, John, he was right there. Paul never left my side the whole time I was sick. He was very concerned about me."

This, of course, was an obsession with Barbara, to test others' concern for her. I decided to place her under hypnosis in an attempt to get closer to the truth.

In a matter of moments Barbara was asleep, but she seemed to be fighting the deep sleep that she had gone into previously. I said, 'Does it bother you to go under hypnosis?"

"I've got too much to hide," she answered, apparently sensing my motivation.

"Are you afraid of telling me something?"

"Yes."

"What are you afraid will happen?"

"What people will think of me. I don't want people to think bad. Because it is not bad. It's just something that happens."

"You're afraid of what people will think."

"Yes. That's dumb. That's really dumb. I know you wouldn't think bad."

"But you think badly of yourself, don't you?"

"I hate myself."

"I know you do."

"I shouldn't though. I'm not that bad a person. Everyone tells me I'm not. I know I'm not. But I can't convince myself. There must be something. Something that even I don't know about me. So many things happened this week. So many things I didn't realize."

"Tell me about it."

"I'm such a bum. I can't believe how bummy I am. I am so low. I embarrass myself. I feel like I embarrass everyone around me. I feel like people can look at me and see everything I've ever done. And they say, 'What a low person.' How could those people stand to be with me? I feel so low."

"What bothered you the most during the past week?"

"My sister Holly rebuking me. She didn't want me around. I care so much about her and she couldn't care less about me. It hurts. It hurts so much. The rest of it was nothing compared to that. And that should have bothered me the least. But it tore me apart."

"How did she rebuke you?"

"She knows about my past. About the dope. About all the trouble I've gotten into. And she feels like— she's always felt that I don't want her to do anything. That I want to keep her in a little prison. You know, don't allow her to go out. You see, my folks pretty much let me raise her because they didn't want to. And she still feels this—you know, kind of parent thing toward me. Like I am out to get her, just like most kids feel about their parents. And I'm not. I want so much for Holly. I would give my whole life if I could do something worthwhile for her. But she rejects me. And she got into trouble. I spoke to her about it. I said, 'Holly, it was your own fault.' I did my best to make her realize what would happen. Then my folks found out."

"What sort of trouble did she get in?"

"They found out she was smoking. They found out she was on pot and taking dope. They were going to turn her in to the cops. But I talked with them—she doesn't know it, but I talked them out of it. They were going to put her in juvenile hall as an incorrigible. I pleaded with them. I made them understand that if they did, she'd end up there forever. They finally said okay. And you know what they did? They grounded her for two days or something like that. A completely meaningless restriction. And she knew it. Then she turned around and blamed me for the whole thing. She said that I told them that she was smoking. Which is so far from the truth. They found the stuff hidden in her drawers. What did Holly expect? She's just plain stupid. I told her if she was going to do shit like that, the least she could do was be careful. But she hasn't got that much sense so she blamed me. Like it was my fault. Then, when I tried to tell her that all she had to do was be a good girl for a couple of weeks and my mom and dad would trust her again, she said, 'I don't want to hear any lectures from you.' "

"How does Holly feel toward your father?"

"She rejects him because he rejects her. The whole family's the same way. My dad never had time for anyone but me. Sometimes my little brother."

"Barbara, I'm going to count you into a deeper sleep, and I'm going to take you back a little way in time. One, you're going. . . ."

"I have a headache," Barbara mumbled.

Barbara was still resisting hypnosis. I had to decide

whether to explore her resistance further consciously, or become more firm and place her into a deeper level of hypnosis. I had a feeling that the latter would not only reveal the reason for her resistance but would provide another key to her cure. I pursued that course. "Okay—I'll get rid of the headache for you." Barbara knows I recognize what she's doing, which actually increases her sense of security. Had she thought she could fool me, she would have felt that I couldn't protect her and also that I wasn't sufficiently concerned with her to probe deeper into her motivation. She relaxed, and I said, "I'm going to count to three and your headache will be gone. One, your headache is starting to leave you now. It's starting to fade out. Your head is feeling better. Two, you're feeling much better, your headache is just about gone. Three, your headache is gone and you're feeling well. Now, tell me, how do you feel?"

"Great. My headache's all gone. You're better than aspirin."

I grinned, and then began counting Barbara into a deeper sleep. She was completely relaxed by the time I reached five and I asked her to tell me about Paul and the very first time they met. After a few moments, she began in a low voice, "Paul comes from a family of eight kids. He missed them an awful lot. We just talked about things that we did in our past, like putting up Christmas trees. Neither of us wanted the holidays to come. He wanted to go home but couldn't. I wanted to go home but couldn't. It was fun talking. He really got to me. Then we went over to my place to smoke some dope only I didn't really want to. Paul smoked too much so I decided to get rid of it and I dumped it on the carpet. It was a thick carpet and it just kind of sank in. Then we pulled my bed out and we lay down and looked out the window. The people next door were throwing furniture out of the top story of the house and we watched them. And we watched the motorcycles.

"After a while, we got up and went for a walk. We walked all over Hollywood. We went down to the *Free Press*—we really had a good time. Then we came back and Paul slept on the floor because I wouldn't let him sleep with me. The next day we got up early. We just walked around. We kept saying we were going to go to Griffith Park but we never got there. We talked about getting jobs, both of us wanted to get jobs, but we didn't get around to that either. I cashed a bunch of checks. I got a whole bunch of money and we spent all of it."

I thought, another demonstration of the impulsiveness and lack of foresight of the psychopath.

She went on, "Then, that night, we were going to hitchhike up to Farrell to see my folks, only I got sick. I was kind of sick, but I wasn't sick enough to go to bed yet. You know, my throat was getting sore. We went down to Coffee Dan's to get some hot tea and by the time we started home I almost passed out. So Paul and another guy carried me back to my room because I was too weak to walk. And Paul stayed there the whole time. He didn't leave me. He didn't sleep at all. He sat up all night with me and the whole next day. Then that night he went out to buy me some soup, but he didn't have any money. So he had to panhandle. And it took him a long time to get enough money just to buy me some soup. But he did. I'll love him forever for it. I was so hungry. It was Saturday night and I hadn't eaten anything since Friday morning. Finally, on Sunday, Paul fell asleep. He had taken care of me all that time.

"The next morning, I said, 'Paul, you had better go,' because I had to call Bob. And Bob would get mad if he came over and found another guy there. So Paul hid all of his stuff and left. Bob came over, and I told him, 'Bob, I'm too sick to stay alone. I've got to have someone take care of me!' My throat was so closed up I couldn't breathe, and I coudn't swallow anything, not even my saliva. I had to spit out my saliva because my throat was so closed up. I couldn't swallow at all. And Bob said, 'Maybe I'll come back tomorrow sometime.' And he left. Just like that—he left. That really tore me up. He walked out on me and I was so sick. After a while Paul came back. I told him to call my parents. I wanted them to know that I was sick. They would know what to do. So Paul went out and called them. When he came back he said, 'They'll be here as soon as they can. They're leaving right away.' "

I wondered about the checks Barbara had cashed and the money she had spent. I questioned her about it and learned that she had cashed checks for about thirty dollars, that the money was hers, that it had been her last paycheck. She had spent most of it on earrings for herself, a belt and a hat for Paul, breakfast, candy, and other incidentals. I questioned her more closely about her relationship with Paul but she insisted that Paul believed every girl and every man should be a virgin on the day that they married, and that, although she would have liked to have had sexual relations with him, nothing happened because he wouldn't permit it. She admitted that she made him sleep on the floor because he wouldn't have relations with her. While she was talking, I noticed that she had begun to frown and move about in her chair uncomfortably and I asked what was troubling her.

"I went to bed with Allan and Ronnie. I told you I didn't. But I did."

"If I recall, those are the two fellows who wanted to go to bed with you together."

"Yeah. And we did."

"Barbara, I can tell you've got a lot on your mind. Let's talk about it because there is no sense holding it in."

"First of all, John, I am very hard-up right now. I want to go to bed with someone. I've never been so hard-up before. I've never wanted to go to bed with someone so badly. In my whole life. Not like I am right now. And, John, I feel very bad about it. I feel very, very low. I feel like a whore. That's what I feel like."

I was being propositioned, which explained why Barbara was using my first name. I decided to use this opportunity to begin to enlighten her about the dynamics of nymphomania. I began by asking a rhetorical question.

"Don't you think that it's natural to want to go to bed with someone?"

"I know it is. But I can't accept it. After all the shit I've been through, it doesn't make sense."

"It does. I'll try to explain it to you. It happens to many girls who have had sexual relations before they reach puberty. Afterward they have a tremendous sexual drive. Sometimes this drive cannot be sated, which is your problem. We are going to try to get rid of it, but it is perfectly natural for you to have it."

"But what if I go through with it?"

"Go right ahead."

"Am I evil because of it?"

"No, no. Don't worry about that. Please—I'm serious."

"It's very difficult, John. It's very difficult."

"If you wish, under hypnosis, I can take the drive away—alleviate it to some extent."

"I don't know if I want that either. John, I've got to be honest. I hate to face it, but I have to. You asked me, I think, if I ever had lesbian thoughts."

"Yes, I asked." I was prepared for something, but not this admission. I encouraged her to continue, "Go on."

"I have them a lot and it doesn't make sense to me when I think about it. I could never go through with it. I could never—I enjoy a man. I don't understand why I have these thoughts. It doesn't make sense. It makes me feel terrible."

"Tell me about your thoughts."

"Sometimes I'll see a girl walking down the street. She'll be very pretty. A nice person. A nice-looking person. And I think, 'I wonder what it would be like to go to bed with her.' Now that's crazy. I'm a girl. Girls don't think things like that. They just don't. It doesn't add up. I don't like things that don't add up."

"When you think of going to bed with another girl, what do you think of doing?"

"That's the crazy part. I think of her the same as a man. The same exact sex acts. That's stupid. It doesn't make any sense at all."

"It does when you consider that you want to get close to your mother. That you need a soft, warm, loving mother. You need a mother and a father. But love for you revolves around sex. If you will recall, fatherly love to you—was sex. The two are equated. Love and sex. Your mother never gave you love. You wanted to be held and you wanted to be loved by a mother."

"What can I do?"

"Well, after a while, you are going to find that you are able to approach a woman and find love from her in something other than a lesbian way. It will be very satisfying to you and you won't be afraid of it."

"Do you really think so, John?"

"Yes. Barbara, you've got to trust me."

"I do trust you. Completely."

"Then don't worry about it."

"I'll try not to."

"We'll take care of it. And other things too. After all, you've been going through this for a long, long time. I believe, soon, you will be able to accept these feelings within yourself. Whatever it is, we'll work it out. But you can't be afraid of your feelings, at least with me. Those are part of you. I accept them. I accept you—that almost sounds patronizing. I don't mean it that way. You see, I don't expect any more or any less—I just accept you. I'm going to tell you something now, and I want you to always remember it. It might be the most important thing you will ever learn in your entire life. The best type of relationship, with anyone, is when both know everything about each other and you accept each other completely—no questions asked. And you have this relationship with me. Perhaps you have it with other people, too—I don't know. And that's what it's really all about. You don't have to take acid. You don't have to smoke pot. You don't have to do anything. You don't have to go from this person to that person.

Acceptance of each other—that's the only thing that counts. It's really what all the kids today are going about trying to do—what they're looking for; the trust between two people, no questions asked."

"That's groovy! That's really out of sight!"

"Okay, it's time now to get back to the old grind. What were we talking about? You were telling me about, I've forgotten their names. . . ."

"Allan and Ronnie."

"Oh, yes. As I recall, when we talked previously about that particular situation, you said they both wanted to have sexual relations with you at the same time. But, it wasn't your bag. But from what you say now, I guess it was. Tell me about it."

"It sounds terrible."

"It sounds terrible?"

"Yes! It sounds terrible to me. It embarrasses me to talk about it. Oh, it *is* terrible! Why don't we talk about something else?"

"Tell me about it."

"While I—while I was going down on Allan, Ronnie was going down on me. God! How could I do anything like that?"

"Because you were interested in it."

"It was horrid. And then—then we changed around."

"You changed around."

"Yes. I went down on Ronnie and Allan was—I hate to say the word—John, I can't say it."

"Yes you can."

"While I was going down on Ronnie, Allan was—fucking me. How could I do anything as bad as that? How could I be such a bum? Oh, God!"

"Do you think you are the only one in the world who has done that?"

"Yes."

"You're not."

"Shit. My husband did something like that one time."

"Tell me about it."

"Bob told me about it after we were married. Him and his friend and his friend's wife. And, you know, while Allan and Ronnie and I were doing it, that's all I could think of. But, you know, Bob didn't even think badly of his friend's wife. I couldn't believe it. If I was a guy, I would think, What a whore. What a slut."

"What did you feel when Bob told you?"

"At the time I thought it was funny. I didn't really believe that anything like that could happen in the whole world. And, yet, it does. It really happens. I found out—it happened to me. But you know one thing I couldn't do?"

"What's that?"

"I couldn't kiss either Ronnie or Allan. I couldn't kiss either one of them. I could not do it. It put them both on a real bummer. But I just couldn't do it. When I realized what they were going to expect—more or less, you know, and what was going to happen, I just couldn't kiss them. They started to kiss me and I turned away. But the rest of it didn't bother me. Now, when I think about it, I see a mental picture of what was going on and—I just couldn't kiss them."

"Is that the first time you had sexual relations with them?"

"No. Do you want to hear something really funny? I had sex with Ronnie in the afternoon and then I went over to Allan's house. How could I do such a thing? It was about twelve hours later—but still, that's funny, that's really funny."

"Who did you like more, as a person—Allan or Ronnie?"

"Allan. He was sincere. I mean Ronnie's whole life is sex. His whole world revolves around it. It's purely a physical thing with him. Whereas with Allan there had to be a mental connection. You have to have conversation and enjoy each other's company. Yet, Allan was very abrupt in sex. Whereas Ronnie was very conscientious."

"I'm not sure I understand the difference."

"Allan thought merely of himself. Whereas Ronnie

thought completely of me. Of my pleasure. Their techniques were completely different. Totally. Absolutely no comparison. I think I've told you about how—I feel it's an animal kind of thing?"

"Yes."

"That was Allan's outlook. It was a physical pleasure merely for the man. And Ronnie—it was an enjoyable kind of pause-that-refreshes type thing, you know. Where you both enjoy it. He wouldn't get any enjoyment out of it if I didn't get any. Yet, I don't understand how he could expect me to go through a thing with—like that, and enjoy it."

"Which one are you talking about—Allan or Ronnie?"

"Ronnie. He was so conscientious in sex that I couldn't understand how he could expect me to go through"—she broke off abruptly, then continued, "... Everything I have, I would give for Ronnie."

"What is so special about him?"

"I don't know. That's what's so screwy. I really don't know. He's the only one for whom I would say, Screw the family—I would give up my family. I really would, for him. I'd marry him right now. It's dumb. Because we are not really that up-tight. We don't have that much of a relationship. But I would. I sure would. It seems very dumb to me even saying it, but I would."

As I had suspected, Barbara was unable to give a reasonable explanation for her affinity for Ronnie. Inasmuch as this seemed to have led, temporarily, to a dead end, I decided to explore just exactly how her mind functioned during intercourse in an effort to discover more about the reason that she was unable to achieve a climax. I began by saying, "I don't want to disgress, Barbara, but I would like to ask you about something you said. I believe you told me that the only time your mind didn't go a mile a minute was when you were with Sean."

"Yeah."

"... But with Allan and Ronnie?"

"My mind was going like crazy. I kept thinking about what I would think about myself afterward. I kept thinking, What if the doorbell rings. Oh, boy, I'm hungry! What we're doing must look like a stag movie. I wondered what anybody would think if they looked in the window and saw us. I wondered if I had remembered to put the milk away. Shit like that."

"You were detached from the entire thing."

"Right. I wasn't really there."

This had been a fruitful approach. My next step was to see whether she connected the detachment during sexual intercourse with that which occurred in the past with her father. "And when you played the love game with your father, did you disassociate yourself the same way?"

"Yeah. I would think about what I was going to wear to the dance that weekend. Or I would wonder if so and so was going to come over to the house. Or I'd better go do the wash when he's finished. I thought of anything, just anything that I could think of."

"Just so you know, one of the reasons you can't have a climax is——"

"Because I can't keep my mind on what I'm doing."

I was very pleased. Barbara and I had reached a turning point in therapy. She had begun to understand the basis of many of her problems. She went on, "I know that with Sean I could climax. I just know I could. He's the only one I've been with that I could keep my mind on what I was doing."

"Yes, but did you?"

"No. But, you see, I had quit my pills. And that came to mind. I would have climaxed. But that came to mind. I thought, Shit, should I tell him or not? And, you know, remember—I think I told you I was pregnant? Well, luckily, I wasn't. But, other than that, that was the grooviest time I ever had in sex in my whole life. I dreamt about it—it was so groovy. It was fabulous. Just fabulous."

"When you were with Sean, you were sniffing Amys, right?"

"That was the first time I was with him—when nothing happened. But the next time, when we had relations, we drank grass tea. It doesn't give you the same kind of high. It's not the kind of high that you can't seem to think what you're doing. Just a groovy good feeling."

"Draw a sexual comparison, if you can, between Sean and Ronnie.

"Ronnie is just as conscientious in sex as Sean, except Sean had no animal look. None whatsoever. He looked like a little kid on a roller coaster. Like he was having the time of his life. I enjoyed it, too, because he was. He didn't have that hungry look like he was going to die if he didn't get it. It was a fun thing, you know. I mean we really had a blast. We went out, completely nude, and sat on the patio. There we were, stark naked, sitting there on the patio, in ice-cold freezing weather. I never had such a wonderful time in my whole life."

"How long ago was this? How long, say—before you met Paul?"

"A week and a half."

"How about in relationship to Allan and Ronnie?"

"I met Allan and Ronnie before I met Sean. Before I went out with him. And after I started seeing Sean— that's when I quit seeing Allan and Ronnie."

"Did you have sexual relations after Allan and Ronnie? After you went out with. . . ."

"Sean?"

"Yes."

"No. I haven't had any sexual relations since Sean."

"Who did you think got you pregnant?"

"Sean."

"I thought it was someone named . . . ah, Cory?"

"No, I thought Cory got me pregnant— Oh, God! John, that's because I was lying to you."

"Why were you lying?"

"That's when I hadn't told you about Allan and Ronnie. And I hadn't told you about Sean. But I did think I was pregnant. But it wasn't by Cory. I knew it was by Sean, if anybody."

A CASE HISTORY OF INCEST

"And you were lying because.... ?"

Barbara shrugged. She didn't know why she had lied.

I questioned her further about her lesbian feelings and she related that in her thoughts she was always the aggressor while in her relationships with men, in actuality, she was passive. At that particular moment, I coughed. I had caught a cold about ten days before and it had left me with rather a wracking cough. Barbara became extremely concerned and tried to exact a promise that I would see a doctor the following morning. When I told her it was nothing for her to be concerned about, she replied, "I can't help it if I worry about you." Before I could comment, she went on, "John, I'm very upset about something."

"What?"

"Well, I called Sean when I got into town earlier today, and asked if he knew of a place for me to stay. After paying the bus fare down here, I had less than a dollar and I couldn't get a place and I asked him if he could think of something. I thought maybe I could stay at his pad but he didn't think that would be too cool. Well, anyway, Sean called a friend of his—his name is Webb—and I'm supposed to go over there when I leave here. And, John, I want to know what you think?"

Perhaps Barbara was asking me, like a good, moralistic father, to say no. And had we been further in treatment, when her conscience was more fully developed, I might have said, "No, you should not stay there." However, I have learned to give a psychopath his head in situations where certain activities might be frowned upon, but are not particularly detrimental to society as a whole. Instead I countered her question with a question, "Is that what you want to do?"

"Yeah. I really want to."

"That's a decision you must make."

"You mean it's all right with you? You won't think bad of me or anything?"

"Barbara, I've told you, I accept you as a person. I'm your doctor, not your minister."

"That's groovy. John, I was so worried. You don't know how worried I was. I mean, here I am going to live with a guy that I've never even met. He won't even be in his pad when I get there. I'm just going to go in and when he comes home—Flash Gordon, I'm there! And he knows I'm going to be there. It's out of sight! I'm going to live in the house of a person I've never met!—that I know absolutely nothing about. But after I started thinking about it, I was worried what you would think."

"You don't have to worry what I think. I accept you. I accept whatever you do. Let's get back to Paul and your dad for a moment. What was Paul's reaction to your dad when he met him?"

"I don't know what you mean?"

"Well, I assume Paul knew about your dad and you...."

"Oh, no! Paul doesn't know about my dad. I never told him. He's the kind of a guy that would have broken my father's neck on sight if he had known." Suddenly, she reached out and said, "John, I feel all alone." I took her hand and asked, "Do you feel alone, or do you feel lonely?"

"Lonely. And I don't like it."

I let Barbara rest for a few moments while I went back and looked at some notes I had made and some questions I had jotted down to fill in some of the blank spaces in Barbara's life. One of them was how and where she had met her husband. I questioned her about it and learned they'd met while she had been living in the house with the five guys and two girls. One of the men was Bob's manager and one day Bob came by to see him and met Barbara. One week later they decided to marry. They set a date, called their parents, and were married three weeks to the day after they met.

"Were there any sexual problems with Bob?" I asked Barbara.

"Before or after the marriage?"

"Well, let's start with before."

"Before, no. After, yes."

"What seemed to make the difference?"

"I don't really know. The legality seemed to mess it all up. Then, too, before we got married, he seemed to care. He was giving. After we got married, he was taking."

"What do you mean, he was 'giving'?"

"He was concerned with me. He was considerate. After we got married, he wasn't. He couldn't care less."

"Did you argue about that?"

"No. I never brought the subject up. I didn't want to hurt him. I was afraid it would upset him."

"Then you never argued with him?"

"No. The only thing we ever argued about was how much coffee to put in the coffeepot or how I was to dry the dishes or how often I had to wash the kitchen floor. That's the only kind of thing we argued about."

"And you did tell him about your father before you got married."

"Yes, the night I met him."

"And he didn't believe you...."

"No, he didn't. But nobody ever did."

"And that's when he sent you to see the psychiatrist, Doctor...."

"... Nillos."

"Yes, Doctor Nillos."

"And he assured Bob that your incestuous problem was a real one, and that's when Bob filed suit for the annulment."

"Yes."

I looked at my watch and couldn't believe how long a session it had been. I counted Barbara into a deeper sleep so she could rest before I awakened her. I leaned back and closed my eyes. I dwelled on the highly unusual responses that Barbara gave while under hypnosis. I was amazed at the tremendous strides we were making in therapy. The mixture of psychopath and nymphomania is one of the most difficult of mental problems to treat. And yet, after this relatively short time I had been working with Barbara, I began to feel hopeful.

Seventh Visit,

DECEMBER 11

Barbara was about twenty minutes late for her next appointment. Before she arrived I had decided not to let her procrastinate about going under hypnosis. The progress she had made in therapy was truly remarkable and I was determined not to let her digress. As soon as she arrived, I kept our greetings brief and started the design of flashing lights. In moments, Barbara was in a deep somnifacient trance. For some time I had been curious about the events that had triggered her telling her mother about her relationship with her father. Having learned that Barbara, as Barbara, would refuse to relate any of the details of what had occurred between her and her dad, I bypassed Barbara and went immediately to Cindy.

"Cindy, I want you to tell me what made you tell your mother about the problem with your dad."

Barbara's response came in the little-girl voice I had heard before. "Cindy knew it was wrong. Very, very wrong. She knew it was wrong even though her daddy kept telling her it wasn't. But she knew it was. Cindy felt very guilty and couldn't live with herself the way it was, so one day when her daddy was out bowling, Cindy went into her mom's room and told her she wanted to talk to her about something very important. Cindy's mother said, 'What is it?' And Cindy said, 'There's a problem between dad and me and I can't stand it anymore. I have to tell you about it.' Cindy's mother was very concerned. She said, 'Well, what's the problem?' And ... and then Cindy told her. Cindy was surprised because it didn't seem to disturb her mother at all. She wasn't even shook up about it. It was as though she had expected it. Cindy's mom said, 'Would you like to tell me about it? How far did it go? Do you know when it started?' Cindy's mom was full of questions. Cindy answered, 'I don't really know. As long as I can remember.' 'What did you and dad do?' Cindy's mother asked. Cindy couldn't say it. She just sat there. And Cindy's mom went on, 'Do you think we ought to call dad and have him come home so we can talk about it?' And Cindy said, 'No. I think we had better talk about it first and then we'll have dad come home. I can't face him right now,' Cindy said, 'I really can't.' Then she started to cry. She didn't know whether she'd done the right thing or not. Her mom asked her more questions. She wanted to know everything there was to know about it. Cindy didn't know what to tell her. Cindy told her some of the things, and then her mom said, 'I think we had better call dad and have him come home.' Cindy tried to leave, but her mom wouldn't let her. She said, 'No, Barbara, you've got to stay and face him.'

"You mean her mom said, '*Cindy,* you've got to stay,'" I interrupted.

"No! No! She didn't! She said *Barbara!* Oh, my God!" Barbara writhed in her chair, twisting in anguish. Her knuckles grew white as she bent over, her hands clutching her shoulders, her body rocking back and forth in pain. Suddenly she stiffened. "This didn't happen to Cindy!" she shouted. "It happened to Barbara! It really happened to Barbara—to me! Everything—everything happened to me!"

Barbara began to cry almost hysterically, her body jerking convulsively with deep sobs. Through her sobs and her cries, she kept repeating over and over, "My God, it all happened to me!" It was fully five minutes before I could continue questioning her. And when I started to use the name Cindy, she immediately corrected me. "No, John—it's all right. There is no Cindy. I know all these things happened to me. You don't have to use the name Cindy again. I think I can face it now."

"When you told your mother the problem, did she believe you?"

"Yes, she believed me," Barbara answered in a low, broken voice.

"Did it seem to you that your mother was ever upset about it?"

"No, never. Well—maybe later on, after Cindy's—I mean, *my* dad came home. When he came in, he wanted to know what was wrong and my mom said, 'I think we had better go into the bedroom and talk.' So we all went into the bedroom and closed the door. My dad sat on the bed and he had a beer and a cigarette. He knew. He really knew. And I think he was relieved that it had finally come out. We sat there for a few minutes and dad looked at me but I couldn't look at him. I got up and I started to walk out, but my mom said, 'No, Barbara, I want you to stay.' And then she turned to dad and said, 'Hank, I understand there's a problem between you and Barbara.' And he said, 'What kind of problem?' And my mom said, 'Honey, it's no use. Don't try to hide it. Let's talk it over.' And he said, 'Yeah, there's a problem but it's nothing we can't handle.' He was afraid of anyone else coming into it. Well, my mom repeated things that I had said and my dad started to deny it but I looked at him and said, 'Dad, don't lie. Please. Not now. I've never done anything in my life that hurt me more than having to tell mom. Please, dad, don't deny it.' I remember I kept saying that I was sorry, but mom kept telling me there was no need to be sorry. And my dad kept looking at me like he wished I was dead. But he knew he couldn't get rid of me that easy—just by wishing. He was very upset. He didn't want to stay in the house so we all got in the car and went for a drive. It was dark already. We drove out to Hampshire Road, out near the park. We parked by a clump of trees and started talking again. After a couple of minutes, dad said that it was all over, he would never touch me again. My mom believed him but I knew damn well it was a lie. He couldn't stop and I knew it. Anyway, we all went home and everything was groovy—just like nothing had ever happened. Mom went to bed, and after she was sleeping, dad came into my room. He started to get angry and I started to cry before he hardly said anything. Then he started to cry and said he was sorry. He swore he would never touch me again or even look at me. He broke my heart because he said he would never say another word to me in any way. But I recognized it as the same old story because any time dad didn't get his way with me he would put me through a living hell. I'd get in trouble for things I hadn't done. He was always on my back about something, and I had found it was easier to give in than to go through all that shit. And there he was, so cold and sarcastic now, that he was never going to talk to me again. And after that, for about three weeks, he didn't speak to me—not one word. He wouldn't even look at me. It was really a bad scene."

"What was said when you parked out on Hampshire Road?"

"Well, my dad hadn't driven out there, my mom had. Dad had bought a six-pack. It was his crutch. Every time he gets upset, he gets a six-pack of beer. Never hard liquor—just beer. I had been crying most of the time, you know—riding out there. I hardly said anything. Actually, nobody had too much to say. My mom was very calm. She was panicky calm—if there is such a thing. My father cried. I asked him if he thought it could be worked out and he said, 'yes.' My mom wanted to know how long ago the whole thing had started, but dad told her he didn't remember. But he reminded her that one time he had tried to tell her there was a problem and ask her for help, but she'd turned him away and laughed at him like it wasn't a problem at all. He ended up blaming her for the whole thing. And that upset her, because I think she remembered the incident.

"I've been meaning to ask you, did your mother ever see the pictures that your father had taken of you?"

"Oh, God, that weird! One night my father was out bowling and I was ready to get into bed when I heard mom yell, 'Oh, my God!' I didn't know what had happened and I ran into her room. I remember I was scared, y'know? Anyway I ran in and there's my mom, going through a drawer in father's dresser. It wasn't like she was digging for anything. She knew right where to look. My father had some medals from the war and he put the pictures of him and me underneath the velvet backing. And she pulled the pictures out. I mean she'd been asleep and suddenly woke up and knew where they were! She turned around and looked at me—it wasn't hate, but more like, 'Oh, Barbara—not really!' I was completely crushed. She ran over and got the Polaroid camera she'd given him for his birthday and she threw it down and started jumping on it. She crushed it. She crushed it flat. And she tore up the pictures. She tore them up into little pieces. She was wild, absolutely wild. She ran to the phone and called my dad and told him to come right home. As soon as he walked in my mom screamed. 'Hank! How could you have? How could you?' And my dad turned to me and said, 'How did she know where they were?' And when I told him what happened he didn't believe me. He was furious. And I mean—this is what he'd do whenever he was caught in something, he'd turn and put the other person on the defensive. He ran out, grabbed his suitcase, packed his clothes, and said, 'I'm leaving. This is the last straw!' And I told him, '*This* is the last straw? You did it. Mom didn't do it!' Because, you see, he had told me he'd destroyed the pictures. And I believed him, which was like stupid shit. And all this time my mom was sitting kind of crumpled on the bed. And she was so—oh, God! So torn apart! And I was trying to comfort her. And he was going through this whole scene, 'I'm leaving' and 'I know you don't really love me' and 'I can't go on like this, blah, blah, blah, blah, blah . . .'

"Can you remember what your feelings were regarding your mother at that moment?"

"I felt like—I don't know, like I had to support her."

"You were supporting her."

"Yeah. She was crushed and it was just like I kept telling her, 'Mom, it's not your fault. You didn't do anything.' Because, you know, John, I don't blame her one bit. Except afterward when she realized that it was still going on and then she didn't do anything about it. Of course, then I had to blame her. I had to hold that against her. But, at that time—if you had seen her, you couldn't blame her. There was nothing but pity."

"You didn't feel, then, that in any way, she was in charge?"

"No one was in charge. It was a big chaotic mess."

"Did she give you any comfort at all?"

"She was very comforting to me."

"Tell me about it."

"Well, she just told me, 'I don't blame you, Barbara,' which, you know, I appreciated because I kind of thought that she would. And she said, 'Now I understand all the things that have gone on in the past.' Then, afterward, she never blamed me for going out and trying—well, I mean, for having sex with the guys. She never blamed me for that."

"You mean, she was aware when you became promiscuous and started having sexual relations?"

"That was about a year and a half later—but, yeah, then."

"Then she didn't say anything to you when, through the years, she suspected that something was going on between you and your dad, nor did she say anything when she found out that you were having sexual relations with boys?"

"She never condemned me for it."

"In looking back at what you've just told me, Barbara, it seems to me your mother was behaving according to her pattern. I believe you told me that your mom was never the one to admonish, or render the spankings."

"That's right—my dad did all the spankings. And he's the one who hit me those couple of times."

"Tell me about that again."

"Well, actually, he spanked me just about every day, but he hit me three times. Once when I called him a bastard, which was really a bad thing to do, but I did it and I don't regret it. And once when I was going to testify against that narco. He hit me twice that time and kicked me a couple of times. And then again when I told him I thought it would be fun to be a prostitute."

"When did you tell him that?"

"Just before I came down to L. A. for the first time. He really blew his mind. And I told him it was all his fault."

"Tell me about that."

"Well, he was saying that the reason I was coming down to L. A. was because I was a nymphomaniac and I wanted to be able to go to bed with every guy I met. And I told him that's what I'd do if I wanted to and there wasn't anything he could do about it. And he said, 'You're going to be the same as Tina—that was his first wife—you're going to be another prostitute just like her.' And I told him, 'Well, I think it would be fun to be a prostitute,' and Flash Gordon—he just knocked the shit out of me. God! He really whacked into me that time. I thought my head was going to fall off."

"Do you know very much about your dad's first wife?"

"Just about everything."

In response to Barbara's question, "Daddy, did you ever love anyone else?" her father had started telling her about Tina when she was quite young—around six. And Barbara had a feeling that a part of him still loved his first wife. She told me that Tina had been the "town prostitute" at fourteen. And that her dad and Tina had lived together for two months before they married. Ten days after the marriage Tina disappeared for a time, and when questioned on her return, simply told her bridegroom that she had been attracted to another man and had spent three days at a motel with him. When Barbara's father complained and asked why she had married him, Tina told him, "Only because you're good in the sack." From everything that Barbara had heard, Tina was a beautiful woman with a fascinating personality. She said that her father had told her that Tina played up to men to the point where wives and girlfriends were jealous of her attentions to their husbands and dates. Barbara also complained that her father was terribly inconsiderate and quite often at home, through the years, harked back to his first marriage, referring to "Tina this"—or "Tina that." She recalled, too, that her father had often, during sex, made the mistake of calling her Tina. Her father's marriage to Tina had lasted for two years, during which time she had slept with any number of men. Among them were his best friends, men from the neighborhood and the building in which they had lived.

After I had finished getting from Barbara all the pertinent information regarding her father's first wife, I scanned some notes I had made prior to her appointment. I found what I was looking for and said, "Barbara, at this point I know that you talked about your problem to a friend of your dad's, Brian Reynolds, to your girl friend, Rozelle, and that you also tried to confide in your brother Stu. I have been wondering if there is anyone else that you told?"

"Yes. I told Frank Dempsey."

"Who is he?"

"A policeman."

"You told a policeman?"

"Yes. Well, he's the probation officer in Farrell. He's a wonderful man. I really dig him. And when I finally went to the police—I told him."

"Did you just walk into the police station and ask to talk with someone?"

"No. You see—he's the juvenile, well—he's the

juvenile something or other. And a girlfriend of mine had had this trouble and her parents kicked her out and all of that shit. Anyway, she told me about him."

"How old were you at that time?"

"Sixteen."

"And what did you tell him?"

"Well, I just told him that my father and I had been involved in incest for as long as I could remember and I didn't want him to prosecute my dad, I just wanted him to take care of him. You know, make him see a doctor or something. And this guy agreed not to make any record of it so that my dad couldn't be prosecuted or get into trouble. Then, of course, he wanted us to come in."

"What was the result?"

"Well, my mom, my dad, and I had to go down there once a week to talk with him. I used to drop in all the time—you know, after school or whatever. Anytime I had a few minutes, I'd go down and talk to him. I told him I smoked pot and I dropped acid and he wasn't—you know, he wasn't shocked or anything. He'd listen and he'd tell me different things like, 'Don't deal in the stuff.' I mean, he could understand it and he even felt that grass ought to be legalized. Which I thought was very admirable of him because I agree with it."

"Tell me about the sessions when you went down there with your mother and father."

"Well, sometimes we'd have to wait, you know—to get in to see him. We'd have to sit out in the lobby and I wouldn't sit next to my father. I'd sit on the other side of my mother. Then I'd go in and talk to Mr. Dempsey and then dad and mom would go in. Then my mom and I'd go in and then I'd go in and then we'd all go in. And it was groovy because he would never tell them what I'd said, but he'd always tell me what they'd said."

"He'd always tell you what they'd said?"

"Uh-huh. Because his job was to protect the juvenile. The victim, as it were—in all cases. Even if it meant both of my parents going to jail. I was to be protected. I was his first concern, which I thought was out of sight."

"And, because you insisted that no formal charges be instigated, your father was never prosecuted."

"That's right. I would not have it."

"Tell me, what was your father's reaction when he found out that you had called the probation officer?"

"He was pissed! Was he ever pissed. He went through the usual scene of packing his bags. I swear, he packs his bags more than anybody I know. But, you know, he never left. Not one time. He's just a big chicken shit. A big blowhard. You call his bluff and there's nothing left."

"Do you love your dad?"

"Very much," Barbara answered.

"Just thought I'd ask."

"Oh, I guess he's got his faults," Barbara said matter-of-factly.

"I would have to agree with that."

"Well, everybody's got their bummers."

"Did he do anything because of his anger at you for having told the police?"

"What could he do? He was scared. He was frightened that he might be put away. I mean, I don't blame him. Incest—that's a twenty-year rap."

"What was your mother's reaction?"

"She was happy about it. Very happy. We were all relieved."

"What triggered you into calling the police at that time? You were sixteen—you had told your mother about the situation two years before when you were fourteen. Why did you call at that time?"

"Because nothing was being done. My dad was still after me all the time. No matter what was said at the house—my dad didn't leave me alone."

"Was there something specific? Were you particularly angry at your father at that moment?"

"No. I just felt he needed help."

"Did he get the help?"

"Yes. Because you see, Frank Dempsey insisted that my dad go to a psychiatrist. And he did. He started to go see a psychiatrist."

"And did that alleviate matters at home to any extent?"

"No. Not really. But at least something was being done to help." Then Barbara, as she had on other occasions, asked a non sequitur. "Did I ever tell you about my nightmares?"

"No. I don't think you've mentioned them. But, as a matter of fact—I have a note to ask you about your dreams. If you had any, and so forth."

"Yeah, I have 'em. I really do."

"Would you like to tell me about them now?"

"Okay."

"All right, I'm going to have you open your eyes and look at the flashing design. I want to put you into a deeper sleep—a deeper sleep than you're now in, so that we can go into your dreams. I'm going to count to three and your eyes will come open—you will remain asleep, even though your eyes are open. You will look at the flashing design. I'm going to count, and as I count you will fall into a very deep, a very deep, relaxing sleep. One, your eyes are coming open. They're opening wide. Two, they're opening wider, and, three, your eyes are open. All right, Barbara, look at the flashing design, look at the colors."

"John, did I ever tell you that I see people in colors?"

"No. I don't understand—what do you mean, you see people in colors?"

"Well, I see them in colors. People mean colors to me."

"Like what?"

"Well, like you're pink."

"And pink stands for what?"

"Pink is love. Pink is understanding."

"That's very interesting. I find that most interesting. Tell me about your colors."

"Red is evil. And red is death. Blue is mystic. Green is a good color—a happy color. Like peace. Yellow is an even—a bubbly color. Like I said, John, you're pink."

I felt she wanted me to follow up her reference to me but I chose not to as I wanted to gain a better perspective of exactly how she related color to people, not only because of its connection with me but with her parents as well. Instead of responding to her remark, I asked, "What color is Holly?"

"Holly is pink. Holly's pink and yellow. She's fabulous. There's nothing better."

"What about your mother?"

"My mother is—she's the only one I see in a combination of colors. No, that's not true—I used to see Bob in a combination of colors too, but I haven't seen him in so long, I don't know what color he'd be now. But my mother is red and blue, which blends to purple. But, sometimes, like around Christmas Day, when she's doing things around the house, she turns pink. My mother's a versatile person."

"And your dad?"

"My dad is—pink. But, sometimes I see him and he's violent black. I don't know if you've ever seen violent black. It's shiny—and that's like—to me it's like looking at a corpse. You know, a dead person."

"Like a corpse, that's what black stands for?"

"Uh-huh. Well, it's different than red though, black is actual dead, whereas red is death—like the act of death."

"What about your girlfriend Rozelle?"

"Rozelle is red."

"How about Ronnie?"

"Ronnie was always frightening to me. Very frightening. Because he's the only one that I've never been able to see in color."

"What about his friend, Allan?"

"He's pink. Sometimes he was green. But mostly pink."

"Ronnie had no color, but Allan was pink?"

"Right."

"And Sean?"

"Pink."

"How about Cory?"

"He was like fuchsia. Like a child. Like innocence."

"And Bob you said was all sorts of colors?"

"Yeah—all colors."

"How about Webb?"

"Oh, he's pink—really pink."

"I almost missed the most important person, you."

"I'm black and red. Solid."

"Black is—dead."

"Dead."

"And red is. . . ."

"Black is dead and red is evil, the act of death. I'm like death for everyone who knows me."

I found Barbara's representation of people by color unique. I had never encountered it before and have not encountered it since. I made a note to research the subject and then proceeded with the session. Barbara looked at the flashing design and I counted her into a very deep sleep. By the time I reached ten, Barbara was perhaps in the deepest sleep she had ever been in. Upon questioning her I learned that the worst nightmare she had ever had had occurred at the age of fourteen. In the nightmare she is eight years old. She said, "In the dream my father's in some kind of branch of the service. Like a secret service thing. And he's a guard in—it's like a lighthouse. It's set up on a high cliff. And it's got glass all around it. It's surrounded by glass. And it's round. And only he and I live there. And down from the lighthouse, down by the cliff, there's a school—except it's like an island. I'm not sure it's an island, but all I can see is land and water and this little place, so, you know, to me it's like an island. And my dog, Maxine—she's a beagle. She's a really cute dog. The kind that looks like she's got a smile all the time. And I go to that school. It's a private school, and it's made out of square bricks and there's a play yard. And the water's edge comes right up to the play yard. And there's going to be an attack from these 'things'—things that you can't see, but what they do is—they strangle you. They can't hit or kill you any other way, but they go for the indentation on your neck. You know, from your shoulders to your neck? And they strangle you. And I know it. And my father knows it. I mean that they strangle you. So he tells me that they are attacking because we can see them from the light from the lighthouse. We see them coming. It's in the afternoon, and all the kids, you know, from the school, are out in the yard at recess. My dad tells me to run down the steps in the lighthouse and tell all the kids to get sheets over their heads so these 'things' can't see the indentations on their necks. So they can't strangle the kids. And I have this sheet over my head with holes in it so I can see, and, you know, it's a ghostlike thing. And I run around the school yard telling all the kids to put sheets on their heads, but nobody believes me. No one believes me because they can't see the 'things.' I tell them they're attacking. And I don't understand why they can't see the big footprints in the sand. Because I can. I yell at them, 'You've got to run! You've got to run! They're coming at you. They're going to strangle you!' But they won't listen, and the 'things' come and they strangle the kids. And all the kids, their eyes fall out of their heads and blood pours out of their mouths. And yet they won't run and get away. All these kids drop like flies. And I go into the dormitory and all the kids are laying there dead. Then I know that the creatures are all over the island—these things. So I run back up to the lighthouse and tell my daddy. And when I tell my daddy, he tells me to go to bed. That he's in contact with Washington and all the States and all the big heads of State all over the world. And he tells me to go to bed. So I go to bed. When I wake up, this brier had grown all round the lighthouse. And the brier has puppies in it. All these faces of Maxine, my dog, and I tell daddy, 'Maxine is outside, and look, she had puppies. You've got to let her into the house, daddy.' But daddy tells me not to open the door. I tell daddy I've got to let her in. But he says no. She can't come in. She has to stay outside. I tell him

A CASE HISTORY OF INCEST

that she'll be hungry and that all the puppies are barking. And Maxine is barking. But daddy won't let me go outside. And he won't tell me why. Then I look at the puppies and at Maxine and I can see that their heads have been broken off from their bodies. And the blood is rolling down around the brier. And the blood and skin and parts of their bodies hang on the brier and the blood runs down all over their fingers. Then I wake up screaming. Just screaming. And when I wake up, I'm half scared to death."

"Did you have this nightmare before or after you dropped acid?"

"Before. Much before. I didn't drop acid until after I was—well, it was November. And I had this dream, well, like four months before that. That was the first time I've had it."

"How often have you had the dream?"

"I'm not sure. But like maybe—once every two weeks. Or maybe three."

"Barbara, you're in a very deep sleep. Now I want you to let your mind drift. Let your mind relax, completely relax. Let your mind drift around the dream. This dream has a meaning in your unconscious mind. I want you to let your mind drift around the dream. I'm going to count to ten. When I reach ten, I want you to tell me what the dream means. I'm going to count to ten, and while I'm counting, your mind is going to drift around the dream and analyze it. By the time I reach ten, you will know the true meaning of the dream. I'm going to count now. One, your mind is drifting around the dream. Two, your mind is drifting around the dream and analyzing it. You're going to know its true meaning." I counted to ten, reiterating almost the same phrases so that Barbara's mind drifted around and searched for the meaning of the dream. When I reached ten, I asked, "Barbara, what does the dream mean?"

"I wanted everyone to die so that my father and I could be alone and happy."

I breathed a deep sigh of relief and gratification. Barbara had truly analyzed the dream to its fullest meaning. I had found in my relationships with Barbara, in talking to her conscious self and her subconscious, that she was exceedingly bright and perceptive. And even though she might not have been able to analyze the dream consciously, and I, as an expert could have, ultimately only her unconscious mind knew the true meaning better than any expert. I wondered if she knew the reasoning behind her analysis and asked, "Do you know why all the children die?"

"Because I felt if they were living, they could hurt me, and hurt me again and again. I wanted these 'things' to kill them. It was the only thing my mind could dream up. And I think it happened right after I'd seen a movie about blobs. I wanted the children to die, and yet, when it began, I knew I was wrong and that I had to stop them from dying."

"You wanted them to die because you wanted the world just for your father and yourself?"

"Yes. But my conscience began to bother me and I knew I couldn't let them die without at least trying to help them. Yet, I was happy in my little world when they did die."

"Do you know the reason that you chose the death by strangulation rather than some other method?"

"I think so. I think it's because I always wanted to strangle my father while he was having sex with me. I remember, while having sex with him, I could see his eyes popping out and blood pouring out of his mouth. And I used to want to strangle Holly. I tried to strangle her any time we got in a fight. And I feel that if I ever kill anyone, it will probably be by strangling them."

"Was your sister symbolic of your father when you would strangle her?"

"No. I was just jealous of her."

"You were jealous of her."

"Yes, because I was afraid my father would start paying attention to her when she started growing up."

"Oh? Then this did cross your mind and you worried about it?"

"Yes. When I was very young. When I was fighting

for affection. I knew I had to fight my mother for his affection. And I just couldn't stand the thought of fighting my sister for it too."

"Is that why you pushed your sister out of the tree?"

"No. I pushed her out of the tree for purely pleasure reasons—you know, kid reasons."

"But when you tried to strangle her...?"

"I meant it then. I meant it."

"Now, Barbara, there are other parts of the dream that have significant meanings. I'm going to count to three—your mind will again drift in and around the dream and you will be aware of other meanings. One, your mind is drifting around the dream. It's analyzing it. Other meanings are becoming clear. Two, your mind is drifting around the dream, other things become clear. Three, things are clear."

"The puppy dogs—Maxine's puppies—were strangled. They were strangled by my mother's hands. My mother wasn't there, but I know her hands strangled the dogs."

"Do you recognize the symbolism of the hands?"

"I'm not sure. I—she didn't like Maxine. She didn't like her at all. But, I don't understand. My mother is very nonviolent. It would have hurt her to kill all these kids—I said kids, I meant puppies."

"Could it have been kids? Her own children?"

"Maybe she didn't want any, but my mom loves children."

"Did she love her own children?"

"She loved us as much as she could. Maybe it wasn't very much, but it was as much as she could."

"Do you think that her hands could have——"

"Only one of Maxine's puppies lived," Barbara interrupted.

"Pardon me?"

"When Maxine had her puppies, in real life, four of them died. Only one lived. A little girl puppy."

"Let me ask what I started to ask before then, in light of this. Is it possible, Barbara, do you think——"

"I know what it is," Barbara interrupted. "In the

dream Maxine is my mother and I'm the puppy and my mom is getting revenge against me. Mom knew that I would run outside to save Maxine and her puppies, in which case I would die. But I know it was all in my dream—in the nightmare. She never felt that way about it really. Not really. John," she went on, "I think there's something I should tell you. I think I have a much better outlook on everything now. I don't know why, but in the past couple of days I've just—well, it's like I've accepted things as they are."

"You're feeling better?"

"Much. I feel much better. You know, inside. About everything."

"That's wonderful."

"And I accept the fact that you're helping me. Helping me a great deal. And that I need help. That I really did need it and I still need more. Until now, John, that is—until I started coming out here to see you, it had really been a game. I knew it was a game. But I couldn't stop playing it."

"I know. I understand and I want you to know we're making progress. I mean that. I think we've made a lot of progress tonight."

I had the feeling Barbara was resisting analyzing her dreams further by employing a device sometimes referred to as a "flight into health." I was, however, determined not to let her digress and said, "I'd like to continue to hear about your dreams. Tell me about some others."

"Well, there's a nightmare that I've had quite often. But it's odd, the first time I had it was when I was babysitting. I babysat for these people, you know, up in Farrell, and they didn't care if I fell asleep because I used to stay over, you know—sleep until the next morning. Well, this one night I had a guy come over. It was the first time I'd ever done that. And I didn't tell them about him. Well, later—when I went to bed, after he had gone, I had this dream. In the dream the people I babysit for are looking at me. They just look at me, and what's strange is I don't have any clothes on. But even though I don't have clothes on, they keep saying to each other, 'My, isn't that a beautiful outfit she's wearing?' And I can't understand it. I think maybe my skin is on over my clothes. That I'm not real—well, I am real, but it isn't me. I can't understand and it frightens me. And I keep thinking, 'I've got to take it off. Whatever it is on me, I've got to take it off.' I want them to know that I'm not fake, that I'm not a phony. I say, 'People! This is me!' But they can't hear me. It's like I'm in—I don't know, a glass. And they're looking through the glass like I'm a freak. And I keep saying, 'I've got to take it off, I've got to take it off.' I look around for a knife so I can take my skin off so that they can see me as I really am. I look around in the glass for something, but there's absolutely nothing in the glass except me. It's like I'm cracking up because I can't get my skin off. Then I start to pull out my hair. I pull it out by the handfuls. My hair is so long that when I pull it out and drop it, it piles up around my feet. Suddenly I have all this hair piled up around my feet—right up to my waist. I'm standing in all this hair and they keep saying, 'Isn't that a beautiful outfit? Doesn't she look lovely in it?' No matter what I do I can't get it off. I even try to take my fingernails off. I pull at my fingernails, trying to take them off. I try to take off anything I can so that they can see there's something else underneath. But I can't get them to see it. Then I wake up."

Barbara, in relating the dream, had more than touched upon its true meaning when she said, "I wanted them to see the real me." This was borne out when moments later she told me that it was directly after having had the dream that she told her mother the problem. Further confirmation lies in the fact that Barbara had had this dream on numerous occasions up until that time and then after having revealed the secret to her mother—revealed *herself* to her mother—she never dreamt it again. I, therefore, didn't have Barbara analyze the dream, for the dream had already accomplished its purpose—the baring of her secret, her soul, her very being to her mother.

The next nightmare she related was one that had occurred with regular frequency from the time she was about eight. In it she related, "My father keeps touching me. Just touching me, like this"—and Barbara touched my arm. "And he won't stop touching me, and while he touches me, he makes snide remarks like, 'You have the cutest ass in town.' And, 'You ought to walk around without any pants on.' And in the dream, he has me take my clothes off and he looks at me. He just looks at me. And he keeps saying, 'Take off everything I touch.' And he touches my blouse and I take it off. And he touches my bra, and I take off my bra. It's like I'm a zombie. And he tells me to take off my pants. Then he touches my pants and I take them off. Then he touches my underpants and tells me to take those off and I do. Then I wake up and it's kind of eerie—because it's like a dream within a dream. Because although I wake up, I'm still dreaming. And then when I wake up from the dream within a dream I feel an urge to kill him if he doesn't stop touching me. And the dream goes on and on and he keeps touching me and then—I don't know how, but suddenly I'm lying across a railroad track and my dad is making love to me. And in the dream we have intercourse. He enters my body and I scream and pray that the train will run me over, so that it will be over with him and I won't have to go through it anymore. What's always strange to me is that I want *me* to die, but not him. The train only runs over me. Not him. I figure, if I die, then the rest of the people involved will be safe and no one will be hurt. It's very strange. Very strange because I want to live so much."

As before, I counted to ten and Barbara went into a deeper and deeper sleep. When I asked her to interpret her dream, she began to cry. She seemed frightened, terrified, and confused as she muttered over and over, "Oh, God! Oh, God! What have I done? What have I done?"

"Barbara, tell me what's happening to you."

Barbara moaned and said, "I didn't want him to

touch me—but yet, I did. I knew what he would want to do. When he said, 'Take off your blouse,' I could feel what he was going to do. I could feel his tongue. It felt warm and moist and full of love. I could feel him deep inside me. But I knew it was wrong and I hated me."

"You hated it but you liked it."

"Yes. Oh, yes! I wanted him to do it, but all the time I had the feeling that someone was watching me and I wanted to die. I thought of a train. I thought of a train going deep inside of me. I thought of a train killing me. I prayed, 'Oh, God! Don't hate me! Don't hurt daddy. He doesn't know what he's doing. Oh, God! Take me, but don't hate me. But, God, I want to live, too. Help me, I don't know what to do. Help me, God. Please help me. I'm so confused I don't know what to do."

Barbara's pain and her pleasure were excrutiatingly intense. Her body was obviously inundated with sexual desire. A part of her mind demanded that she obey her father, yet another part of her mind, equally intense, implored that she honor her mother. But most painful of all was the terror rising from the depths of her conscience, threatening her with eternal damnation.

The roar of the train represented the awesome voice of God. Decapitation is punishment. And because Barbara had lost love for herself, the love of her mother and the love of God, her only salvation lay in preserving the love of her father, perverse as it was. And that explains why she wanted to die and her father to live.

I sat for some minutes, thinking how deeply she had searched her unconscious for the interpretation and marveling at the results. I realized, too, that Barbara's personal insight and intelligence were of paramount importance in obtaining them.

After letting her rest I continued with the session, "Barbara, the dreams you've told me about thus far occurred primarily before you told your mother the secret. I'd like to know about the dreams you had after you told her."

"I've dreamt mostly about hanging myself."

"Mostly about hanging yourself."

"Uh-huh. And I hang myself in the most fantastic places. Like off of bridges. In cars. I often dream about hanging myself from the light in a car. I think it'd be out of sight if somebody found me like that. And yet, in my dreams when I hang myself—I'm never distorted. I'm not distorted and I always have my best clothes on. Like somehow hanging myself will finally give me recognition or something. That people will finally see how crushed I am by the whole thing. But I guess I don't want to look bad, that's why I'm so dressed up. I want people to think I'm pretty even though I'm dead. I want them to be sorry I'm dead."

"Who do you want to be sorry?"

"People I don't know."

"People that you don't know?"

"Uh-huh."

"That's very interesting."

Barbara had other dreams—nightmares—that were also death-oriented; however, their significance was not as great as those that I have related. Barbara started to tell me about one dream but couldn't decide whether it had been a dream or one of her trips. I regressed her and, although there was even confusion in her subconscious as to its nature, I finally ascertained that it had been a trip. A most interesting trip. And, while still under hypnosis, I had Barbara relive it.

"I had dropped a Blue Mist, which is a groovy trip. As far as I'm concerned, it's the best trip you can have because Blue Mist is just heroin—no other stuff in it. There's no speed in it—no rush. It comes on real soft, and when you—it's like climbing up a bunch of stairs and ending up on a cloud. It's really groovy. It's an easy thing. You don't get tired. Most trips make you tired or they make you rush or they put you on a bummer. But Blue Mist is the grooviest thing I ever had in my life. It cost twenty a tab, which is outrageous because most acids cost like five or six. Anyhow, I dropped it and I was just sitting on my bed and—as I recall, it was my fourth trip. The fourth trip

I had ever taken. And in it I was walking—everything was black and there was like a road with a white line down the center, a broken white line. And it was like I had to walk. And I came to a stop sign, you know, like traffic warnings? And the sign said, 'Caution, Pain ahead.' I walked on and I saw people—all the people that I had caused physical pain—they were standing, each of them in the situation—you know, the situation where I had caused them the pain."

"Who were the people that you saw?"

"Holly, my sister, and other little kids that I knew when I was a kid—kids I had grown up with. And people—some of them I didn't even know, like in school, you know, throwing a rock at somebody or something like that. And I walked on and what was odd was—it was like they couldn't see me, like they were doing their own thing and they couldn't see me but I could see them. I kept walking and walking up this, you know, black road with the line down the center and I kept coming to signs, just like the first one. I kept going and then I came to a sign that said, Caution. Do not look back, do not turn back.' Then more signs that said, 'Greed; Hate'—just everything that I had done to anyone that was bad. And I kept walking and walking until I came to the end of the road. It was a very, very long road. And they had all those signs on it. Some of the signs overlapped the others, like 'Mental Anguish' and 'Physical Anguish' and 'Physical Pain,' you know—they might be stacked one right next to the other like I would not only hurt my sister's mind, I would also hurt her body. Like selfishness toward others—yet I never saw anything, not one scene where anything was hurting me. I only saw things where I had hurt other people. Then, when I came to the end of the road, there was a red light and there was another sign but this one said, 'Curves ahead.' And right next to it was another sign and it said 'Future ahead.' Everything was black but suddenly a green light turned on and I started ahead again and in a flash the sky was blue. The whole world turned blue. And there was nothing but beautiful things. Things like flowers and trees and grass. And wonderful things like bunny-rabbits—and they were all blue. They were out of sight! A blue bunny-rabbit! Wow! And now the road was smooth when before it had been full of chuckholes. And where there had been curves, there weren't curves—it just stretched straight out in front of me. And I walked over it. I kept walking and walking until I came to steps at the end of this blue road. And I started up the steps and a blue light shone down on me and blue is the sign of mysticism. And I walked up the steps, there were so many, and there was a thing like a pagoda at the top. And when I got to the top, I was in the pagoda and my girlfriend Rozelle—the one that had caused me so much pain—she was on a trip too. Only hers was a bummer. And when I got inside the pagoda, a voice, a big voice—said, 'Beware of Rozelle. She brings you only pain.' And then it said, 'Now is the time for sleep. Relax. Go to sleep.' So I lay down and I went to sleep. But as I was lying down, I looked at Rozelle and a ghostlike thing left Rozelle and walked across the room and through the wall and was gone. Then I fell asleep. That's all that I can remember about the trip. It was the grooviest one I'd ever been on. But the next day the shit really hit the fan."

"How?"

"Well, just like on the trip. Like I was warned—Rozelle told my dad that I had screwed every guy in town and she named them. She also said that I was a big whore and that I took dope and—just everything. She said all these terrible things about me just like the voice on the acid trip had told me it would happen. After that, every trip I've been on—at the end of the trip, I see this pagoda scene and I'm forewarned of the future."

"Barbara, think about this for a moment, do you feel that the Blue Mist or any of your acid trips has done anything good for you?"

"Very much so," she answered without hesitation.

"Could you tell me what you think it's done?"

"It's caused me to be more receptive to things about me. Before I used to just kind of shut out the world and say it's not there—and what I did see were only the bad things. Then, there was nothing groovy in the whole world. I couldn't even see a reason for wanting to live—for wanting to be anything. I figured, shoot, I'm here today and gone tomorrow. So I figured there was nothing really to work for. But after I started dropping acid, I started looking at myself and seeing that there was something there. That maybe in some way I could help somebody else and if I could do that—then my life wouldn't be such a waste. I found, too, that I had confidence in myself. I didn't get hassled over little things anymore. I didn't want to hurt anyone. And I didn't have fear anymore of—well, little things. Like I had been afraid of the dark and after I dropped acid, suddenly I wasn't afraid of the dark anymore. I realized that dark is the same as light, only there isn't any light there. And what's going to happen to me at night is going to happen to me in the daytime. This one trip bettered my entire life. It made me more receptive to love. And I got to feeling that I wanted everyone to love me—for everyone to think highly of me. Before, I'd say, 'Frig the world,' and I meant it; now I say it in kind of a half-assed way, because I really do care. I don't want anyone to think badly of me. Unless I've done something to deserve it."

"Some people feel, after dropping acid, that they became closer to God, or they've had an intense religious experience. Do you feel that?"

"No, I think God is in yourself. You feel it in yourself or you don't feel it. I don't believe in a church. I feel that a church is a thing made up in men's minds. It is a crutch for them to lean on. I don't believe in church. I don't believe in giving *my* money so they can build a bigger church. Why don't they just go under a tree? That's what God made. God never made a church in this whole world. He didn't go—Flash Gorden, there's a church. But he did go—Flash Gordon, there's a tree. He put life in a tree and we can't do that. I feel like if I walk outside and there's a bird singing and the rain's falling, I'm closer to God than standing in any church saying Hail Marys and all that stuff. I don't believe in it. But I do feel that I believe in God within myself. I think God is my conscience."

"Have you ever read *The Pilgrim's Progress?*"

"*The Pilgrim's Progress?* It sounds familiar—but, no, I don't think so. What's it about?"

"It's about a trip."

"Is it really? What kind of a trip? Like the Mayflower?—or like one of my trips?"

"A little like one of your trips," I answered.

"Tell me about it!"

I had read *The Pilgrim's Progress* when I was around sixteen and I had to stop and think for a few moments. "As near as I can recall," I began, "It's a dream about man's journey through life to the celestial city, or heaven—in your dream it would be the pagoda. And the dream is about all the pitfalls and temptations that he meets. Sometimes they are represented by persons with names such as Sloth"—I really had to search my memory—"Presumption, or Hypocrisy, and sometimes by physical entities such as the road of danger or the low country of conceit. And sometimes the persons are helpful, such as Prudence and Piety; sometimes the places are helpful, such as the Valley of Humility. But as I remember it, there were pictures, and in the pictures there were always signs pointing the way."

Barbara's eyes opened wide. "You're kidding! I've never read that book."

"Are you sure?"

"Positive. But I'm going to get it. It sounds like my bag."

I looked at my watch and was surprised to see that it was past midnight. I had already scheduled Barbara for an appointment for the following evening so I concluded the session by letting her sleep for five minutes. Before awakening her, as I had done in the past, I erased all conscious memory of the things we had discussed.

Eighth Visit,

DECEMBER 12

"John, what if everything I've told you is a lie?"

Barbara was sitting opposite me, pale and shaking with anxiety. Just before leaving the office the preceding night, I had told Barbara that I planned to give her several tests at this meeting, to determine the depth of her hypnotic trance. I had had no idea that it would shake her up so much. She told me she'd practically not slept the entire night and had gone around the entire day anxious and concerned about the tests. She assured me that she wanted to tell me the truth, but that since what she had said, she had said under hypnosis and couldn't remember, she had no way of knowing if it was the truth or not. And she was afraid that she had lied. I pointed out that most people lie to some extent and whether or not she lied was unimportant. The fact was that I accepted what she said and I felt I knew when she was exaggerating or lying. I told her, "I accept you."

"But if I've lied, then I can't accept me."

"Then you'll have to change that."

"But it bothers me deeply, John. It just kind of hit me today that I've lied a lot in my life and—I don't dig it."

"If you really don't dig it, then starting today you should change it."

"But I've got to make up for what I've already done."

"No, you don't have to make it up. Just, from now on, tell the truth, if that's what you want."

"But why do I lie?"

"Tell me one lie that you've told me."

"That's just the point. Snap, dab. Right there. I don't know what lies I've told you because I don't know what I've said."

"Then you don't have anything to worry about."

"But I know *me*. I must have lied. And I feel guilty about it. I feel like a real shit."

"Barbara, there's no sense in feeling guilty about it. That gets you out of the obligation of being responsible for what you do."

"I don't understand."

"You do something that you want to do. That's a selfish motive. Then you flagellate yourself by feeling guilty. You know, you say—'Oh, I'm a terrible person.' That, you see, gets you off the hook so that the next time you can do exactly the same thing and then later, you can feel sorry and guilty about it."

"But I don't want to do that. I want to know why I lie. When it really doesn't—" she broke off, but quickly continued, "Really and truly, I've had a screwed up existence, but there's no need to lie."

"A lot of your lying is called, 'wish-fulfillment fantasies.' You say what you wish will happen. Some of it is to impress people. Some of it is hostile, in a way. You know you're fooling someone and putting something over on them, which makes you feel better than they are. So all of these things tend to——"

Barbara interrupted, "But what makes a person do that?"

"Insecurity, because you don't accept yourself."

"Shit! I used to lie when there was no reason in the world to lie. And I don't dig it. I feel like I've got to do something to make up for what I've done."

"Don't lie anymore."

"John, will you do this for me? If, when I'm under

hypnosis, if I lie—will you say, 'Barbara, are you lying?' "

"If you're really sincere, you won't lie anymore. That's all. If it's that important to you, then you just won't. I'm not asking you for any promises because it wouldn't make any difference. You could tell me that you're not going to lie and then lie your head off. The only thing that that would do would be to make you feel guilty and make you pull away from me because of the guilt. And, if you look back at your relationships with people, you know how your guilt can mess them up. I'm not going to let you do it to ours."

"You're not?"

"No, it's all right to lie to me. You don't have to run away."

"But it's not all right."

"Then it's up to you to change. But you can't run away because I condemn you for it. If you run away, it will be of your own doing entirely."

"My own guilt."

"Yes. You won't be able to put the blame on me."

"I'm not trying to. It's just—it's been a really freaky thing with me today."

"That's good, Barbara. When you can come to somebody and say, 'Hey! I've lied to you,' that's fine. I think that shows a good deal of trust."

"Yeah, but I don't know what I've lied about."

"That's all right. I do."

I asked Barbara about her reading habits and learned that while she had read a great deal during her years in school, she had not since that time. I learned, too, that she had dropped out of high school in the eleventh grade, just five weeks before going into the twelfth, and had obtained her high school diploma in night school. She stated that she dropped out because she couldn't communicate with the other kids.

"Why didn't you like the other kids?" I asked.

"I just didn't like them. I felt very inferior around them—they all had groovy clothes. I didn't have groovy clothes. And they dated the guys in school. I never did. I dated very little in school."

"Why?"

"I don't know. I was afraid. I was very shy. Like when everyone else was out gossiping and eating lunch together—I used to take my lunch and go some place else like the biology room, just not to be around the other kids. I loved my biology room. I really did. I used to cut up frogs and dissect things and my biology teacher and I got along very well." Then, the non sequitur. She said, "John, hitching out here tonight I wondered if the reason I became such a liar is because of my dad making me keep the secret for all those years."

"I think that's a very definite part of it. I've been very impressed that you kept your father's secret for as long as you did. It generated a tremendous pressure on you. A pressure to spill something. Like—Newton's law that every action has a opposite and equal reaction." That's the way the human body is built. When you put pressure one place, it comes out another. If you keep your emotions down it comes out in an ulcer or some other physical symptom."

"You mean, something's got to give somewhere?"

I nodded and leaned over and threw the switch that turned on the flashing lights for the color design. Barbara immediately became apprehensive and said, "John, I don't want to be put under hypnosis tonight."

"Because you're afraid to find out that you've lied to me?"

"Absolutely."

"Do you trust me?"

"Now I do. Completely."

"Then, look at the flashing design and as I count to ten your eyelids will become very heavy and you'll fall into a sound, deep sleep One—" Even as I had begun to count Barbara's eyelids closed.

I used several tests that I have devised to determine the depth of hypnosis that a subject attains. The depth of Barbara's hypnosis was a complete somnifacient trance. When I concluded the testing I asked her, "Have you lied, at all, about your father?"

"No. I did not. Not at all."

"Are you lying now?" I asked.

"No. I am not lying now. I haven't lied in anything I told you about him and our relationship."

"I believe you told me, some time ago, that you had achieved a climax while you were stoned on acid."

"I think that was more of a mental climax—I mean, I was peaking on the acid. And it's like a climax, your mind's flying with a million thoughts, then there's a breakthrough, a relief, because you're constantly going up and it's almost to the point where you wish it would hurry and end because at times it's a painful thing—in your mind. An exhausting thing. You're racing so fast you get exhausted and you wish it would hurry and peak out so it could go down. But, John, I've climaxed for real since then."

"Oh? Tell me about it."

"With Webb. And you know what else?"

"No, what?"

"I enjoyed kissing him. I really dug it. I never thought I'd like kissing any guy, but I—I don't know. Maybe it was him, but we had a groovy time kissing and everything."

"And all this has occurred within the last few days, since you returned to L. A."

"Uh-huh. I'm so proud of me." Barbara said with a wide grin on her face.

I had to laugh at Barbara's attitude. She was proud and, also, embarrassed to some extent. Obviously her enjoyment in kissing a man was a significant step forward in her therapy. And, although she didn't recognize it, achieving a climax had deeper meaning than Barbara imagained. Many women go through their entire lives without attaining a climax. And Barbara, though her life had been fraught with emotional distress, was well on the road back to mental health. But it was extremely important for Barbara to know the reasons why she had achieved physical enjoyment. "Barbara," I began, "I'm going to count to five and you're going to know why—and understand, why you can have a climax now whereas before you could not. One, you are going into a deeper sleep. Two—your mind is becoming clearer. Three, you're much more relaxed, you're going deeper and deeper into your unconscious. Four, you're going to understand why you can climax now. Five, please tell me—"

"I can climax now because when I was back home my father repulsed me. Before that, I still loved him—I still enjoyed the idea of having sex with him. I couldn't get him out of my mind when I was having sex with someone else. I thought of him constantly, no matter who I was with. I could not forget him—I really couldn't."

"What kind of thoughts did——"

"I didn't have bad thoughts about him," Barbara interrupted, "it was like a love. That I shouldn't make love with anyone else. But now I can. He turned me off so much while I was up there, by rejecting me. My whole family rejected me. Now I can relax and enjoy sex. Enjoy it completely."

"And how do you feel in general?"

"I feel much better. I even feel healthier."

"Do you think that the climax is a sign of that?"

"Yes, I do, I have a better attitude—even when I'm mad or upset about something, I still have a better attitude. And it's not the depression thing I was in. Especially when I first came to see you. But lately I haven't had that feeling at all. Even though I was depressed today, very depressed, it wasn't the same sort of thing. I feel it's the kind of depression that anybody can get into, whether they've got big problems or not."

"And you were depressed today because you felt you had been lying."

"Right. But I honestly think, John, that it was a normal feeling and I never used to have normal feelings. I mean, let's face it—before this I had had a thousand and one excuses why I would not have been here tonight. And I'm being honest. I wouldn't have been here come hell or high water. Even if it meant going back to Farrell—I wouldn't have been here. That's how scared I was. Truly."

"Are you frightened now?"

"No. Not a bit."

"Your father did make passes at you then while you were at home?"

"Like every five minutes."

"And did you give in to him?"

"No. I did not."

"Did you want to?"

"No."

"Good. Now, let's review what went on between the time when you arrived in Los Angeles and when you met your husband, Bob. Tell me about the people—the men, that you met during that time."

"You mean the guys that I went to bed with?"

"Okay, we'll talk about them."

"Well, let me see—there was one, two, three—three guys."

"Okay, tell me about them."

"—no, four! Four, or maybe it was five? I'll have to think about it."

"We'll get to all of them. Start with number one."

"Well, I had come to L. A. with the intention of living with a band, you know, a group, called the Flip Side. They were playing at a place out on the Pacific Coast Highway. You see, I had met the group when they were up in Farrell. I kind of got to know all the guys and I really dug them and they grooved on me. I mean there was no sex or anything. We were just all very good friends, and when I told them that I was planning on leaving home, they thought that I might be able to, you know, keep house for them, take care of their clothes, and all that kind of shit. Anyway, by the time I got to making up my mind to leave, they'd left to play the gig down here. It took me a week to get enough money together for my fare and when I showed up, they were really glad to see me. There were five guys in the group and I moved in with them. But it didn't work out because—well, they only had a two-room motel suite and there wasn't any kitchen or anything, so there was no cooking to do and with the five of them living in the two rooms—it was just too much. I slept with a different guy each night and honest, John, I didn't have sex with them. They were just like brothers. But it was obvious that I couldn't go on living with them in the two rooms so when Mark—he was their manager—said I could stay at his place, I accepted. And he's number one, the first guy I went to bed with."

"Tell me about Mark."

"Well, he was around twenty-five, single, and when he took me over to his pad, he made all these wild promises. You know, how he was going to make me a star and bla, bla, bla, which I didn't pay any attention to because I knew it was a bunch of shit. Anyway, at the time, I was very upset because I got kind of hung up on the bass guitar player in the group, Manny, and I knew I wasn't going to see him for a while because they were going to go on the road. Anyway when we got to Mark's place there were these two girls—well, and——"

"Hold on a second," I said, "is this the group of people that you told me about previously? Where the girls panhandled and gave you money and where you didn't have to do anything while you lived there?"

"Yeah! That's cool! I mean, you remembering that."

"You said too, I think, there were some other guys living at the house but that you didn't have anything to do with them."

She hesitated a moment, and said, "That isn't the truth, John."

"You did have something to do with them then?"

"Uh-huh. I guess I lied. That's what I mean—I don't know what I've lied to you about."

"We're getting at the truth now. Just tell me about it."

"Well, Mark has this groovy, little three-bedroom house up in Hollywood, and his brother, Larry, and another guy named—I think his name was Carl—lived there with the two lezes. Anyway, I was very upset that night—the first night I was there—and they showed me where I could bed down and later when Mark came in I was crying. He asked me what was wrong, and I told him that I was lonesome for Manny. And he said, 'Well, you won't be lonesome for long baby.' And he went on with, you know, bla, bla, bla, the whole scene. Anyway he made his little play and I put him down—I put him on a real bummer. I told him that I didn't come there for that kind of shit and that I wasn't going to do anything and well, you know—well, anyway, after a couple of days I went to bed with him. Then Larry came in one night while Mark was gone and I went to bed with him. The next night I went to bed with Carl and then a couple of days after that another guy showed up—I think his name was Steve. I didn't really know him. We just talked for a couple of minutes and I don't know—we went to bed. Then, right after he balled me, you know, he got up and left and that's the night I met Bob."

"I'm interested in why you went to bed with Mark."

"Because he was nice to me."

"Okay, how was he nice to you?"

"Well, he hadn't made me clean the house or anything but he made the other girls do it. And he made them go out and panhandle for money for me. So I figured he thought I was something special."

"And why did you go to bed with Larry?"

"He was Mr. Nice Guy. He was about six feet tall, maybe a little taller, and he had blond hair and blue eyes and kind of an angelic face. He was very well built, he really was. I mean any woman would have to look at him twice. I used to call him 'Angel' and I used to call Mark, 'The Bastard.' "

"Why was that?"

"Mark looked slimy. He looked like a snake, like he was always conniving to get something out of somebody. And the more I talked to people who knew him, the more I realized he was a shit. You know, like all that malarkey he fed me. He was going to take me to the best restaurants, to the best places in town, and introduce me to all kinds of people. He never did. And yet, while he didn't do that, he treated me better than the other girls that were there. He really did."

"How about the other fellow you mentioned, Carl? Tell me about him."

"Carl was gicky. He was horrid. I don't know why I went to bed with him. He was kind of, you know—the kind where every other word is 'baby.' Stuff like that. He made me sick. I couldn't stand him."

"Barbara, I'm going to count to five and you're going to be able to tell me why you went to bed with Carl. One, you're going into a deeper sleep and everything is becoming clearer. You're getting more insight each moment. Two, you're in a deeper sleep. Three, much deeper, still deeper. Four, everything is crystal clear now, and five, you can tell me."

"I was very lonely. One day Carl was nice to me. He didn't seem his cocky self. He was sincere. He talked about things he'd like to do and things he'd like to be. I went to bed with him because, for one moment, he was sincere."

"And Larry, why did you go to bed with him?"

"He was just a nice guy. He wanted to ball me and I figured, "What the hell." It wasn't going to kill me and he'd enjoy it."

"You felt you were doing him a favor."

"Yes. I couldn't have cared less."

"Who did you enjoy going to bed with the most—Mark, Larry, or Carl?"

"Larry because he was sincere and a nice guy all the time. But Mark was better in bed. And—" Barbara stopped talking and when, after about thirty seconds, she didn't continue, I asked, "And, what?"

"There was another guy that I went to bed with but I don't remember his name. Isn't that terrible, I went to bed with him and I can't even remember his name."

"Barbara, I'm going to put you into a deeper sleep and you will remember his name. You're going back now, one, you're going back in time. You're going back to that time of your life. It was around the time that you knew Larry and Mark and Carl. Probably just before you met Bob. You went to bed with someone. What was his name?"

"—I, I never—I never knew his name. He knew my name, I told him my name, but I didn't know his. How could I have done that? How could I have balled a guy without even knowing his name? I was so low. God, how could I?"

"How did you meet him?"

"He came jogging past me one morning. I had seen him a couple of times jogging in the street. Going past Mark's place. He was blond and he wasn't much taller than I was. He was really neat. We started talking and we went over to his house. He was a health nut and he made this thing out of apple cider and orange sherbet. It was kind of like a freeze. God! Was it ever good. We talked about a lot of things—you know, how he went jogging and swimming every morning and every afternoon—the whole bit. And we went to bed."

"During all this time, were you worried at all about becoming pregnant?"

"No. I was on birth control pills."

"How long had you been on the pill?"

"Since I was fifteen."

"Who gave you the prescription at that age, if you got them from a prescription?"

"Well, I had been going to this doctor, since I'd been around eleven, you know a Navy doctor—because my dad had been in the Navy—and I'd been going to him at that time for a vaginal infection. He was the doctor that Frank Dempsey, the juvenile probation officer, had sent my dad to see, and he knew about my dad's messing around with me. So when I told him I wanted birth control pills, he thought it might be a good idea. He gave me a refillable prescription. He was a groovy doctor, an out-of-sight guy. I really appreciated him. I loved him to death for it."

"I'd like to talk about the two girls that lived at

Mark's house. And Barbara—this is truth time. How did you know they were lesbians?"

"They told me."

"They told you that?"

"Uh-huh. The first night that I got there."

"How did that make you feel?"

"Sick."

"Did you feel any attraction at all toward them?"

"A little."

"Did that frighten you?"

"No. Because I had no intention of going through with it. I mean, they made this half-assed pass at me and I turned them off. They knew what the score was, I wasn't buying."

"Tell me about the pass."

"Well, this one night I was lying in bed reading and Diana came in and sat down next to me. We chatted for a few minutes and then she put her hand on my ass. And I said, you know, 'Cool it—I don't make that scene.' And she said, 'Really, don't you?' And I said, 'No. I don't dig it. No way.' And that was it. After that, we became pretty good friends and we used to laugh about it. I thought it was hilarious."

"Tell me about Bob. I think you mentioned that he had a homosexual problem."

"Yes, he had—well, he swung both ways for a while, but I don't think he'd done that for the last, maybe eight to ten years."

"Do you still miss him?"

"No. I think about him every now and then. But I don't miss him. Not anymore. But I'd still like to get my wedding gifts back from him."

Our eighth visit was over. I counted Barbara into a deeper sleep, erased all conscious memory of the evening's session, and after ten minutes awakened her. We went out for coffee and it was close to two when we parted. Barbara had come in at ten. Those four hours marked a crucial point in the therapy.

Ninth Visit,

DECEMBER 19

"... so I moved out."

"You've left Webb?"

"Yeah. On Saturday. I got my things together and moved out."

"Why?"

"Well, last Thursday—I think that was the fourteenth—Webb told me that he was going out. That he had a date. Well, I just don't dig that shit. I mean—here we are, living together, you know, like any other married couple and he has a date with another girl."

"You were living together like any other married couple."

"Well, of course—John, you know what I mean. Obviously we weren't married. But, we had gotten pretty close and we had talked about marriage."

I didn't say anything but waited for Barbara to continue. After a moment she said, "No, John, that's a lie. We didn't talk about marriage. I mean, I guess I'd been thinking how nice it would be to be married to Webb. I was really hung up on him. I really dug him. But deep down I knew nothing could happen between us. You know except—for what was going on."

I found Barbara's ability to distinguish between her fantasy wishes and reality encouraging, but decided against pointing it out here. Instead, I said, "Did you fight?"

"No. I began to feel like I was intruding and on Saturday I got my things together and I went up to Sean's."

"Is that where you're living now?"

"No. I'm living with Walter."

"Walter. I don't think you've told me about him."

"I couldn't tell you about him. I just met him two days ago. You should see him, John, he's out of sight. He's the grooviest guy I've ever met. You know, like I just admitted, Webb didn't talk about marriage with me, well—Walter has. He wants to marry me."

Obviously, there were some things about Barbara that hadn't changed and which were not so encouraging.

"Tell me about him."

"When I left Webb on Saturday, I—like I said, I moved up to Sean's. I stayed overnight and on Sunday morning some friends of his dropped in. Walter was one of them and—I don't know, we just hit it off right away. He and his sister have this little house down near Hollywood and Western and when he asked me if Sean and I had a thing going, I told him, 'No. I'm just staying here because I have no place else to go and Sean really doesn't want anybody around all the time.' Well, Walter said that he'd come back and pick me up later, around three, and I could live with him and his sister. I thought he was putting me on, you know, just saying it. Then when four o'clock came and passed, I really didn't think he was going to show up. But at four-thirty, or maybe a couple of minutes past that, he came and he had his sister, Sandy, with him. And, John—it's really groovy. Sandy is a doll. I just love her to pieces. She's a secretary somewhere or something. And Walter—he doesn't want me to work or anything. And this afternoon he bought me two outfits. This is one of them."

Barbara was wearing a handsome pants suit. After I commented on how well she looked in it, she went on, "And he doesn't want anything of me—just me. He's a salesman—so his time's his own. He earns real good money and he wants to spend it on me. John, I'm so happy!"

"Now let me understand, you moved in with Walter and his sister yesterday afternoon."

"Right. And they have this two-bedroom house and Sandy has one bedroom and Walter and I have the other one."

"Is Sandy married?"

"No. She's just about a year and a half older than I am and she's really out of sight. She's groovy. We have the best time together. We sat up all night talking."

"Walter, I take it, is single?"

"He's divorced. Laurie, that's his ex-wife, she really put it to him in the seven months they were married. Boy, he went through hell with her. They've been divorced now for five months, and Walter told me that until yesterday he didn't think he'd ever get married again. But last night he said that if he had married me instead of Laurie, he'd still be married."

"Did you tell him anything about your personal life?"

"You mean about my dad? Yeah, I did."

"What——?"

"And," Barbara interrupted, "I told him about coming out here, you know—for therapy."

"What was his reaction when you told him about your dad?"

"Well, like—he didn't believe me at first. But I told him I wasn't lying. Then, when I told him about seeing you because of dad, I guess that convinced him and he got very mad. You know, he said he'd heard about incest but didn't believe it really ever happened. That is, he believed it, you know, if an uncle and niece were involved or maybe a brother and sister but when I told him it was my own dad—wow. That tore him up."

After listening to five more minutes' praise of Walter's virtues, I managed to digress and asked, "When is the last time that you dropped acid?"

"Last July. Just before I came down to L. A."

"How old were you the first time you dropped any?"
"Fourteen."
"Tell me about it."

"I was in the tenth grade and—no, it was the ninth grade—and this guy, Kenny, told me he had some stuff called green wedges and that it was the best stuff around. It was pure acid. He said it made your head do things like grass—even more than grass, you could see things. Anyway, Kenny came over to my house, my parents had gone away for the weekend, you know, and Rozelle was spending the night with me, so Rozelle and I split the one cap. I wasn't scared or anything but my God, Rozelle—she was freaky. She was afraid to take it or do anything because she heard that—well, Rozelle's aunt was a nurse and she had told Rozelle something about acids and what they could do to your children if you ever had kids. But I wanted to find out what it felt like, so when I was sure my parents had really gone I dropped the acid. So help me, I really thought it was a lot of shit, everything that Kenny had told me—you know, that I was going to see things. Anyway, I dropped the acid, and I and Rozelle were sitting on the motorcycles out in the garage and I was watching a beacon light over at the airport. The light's on a tower and, as I was looking at it, I could have sworn the tower was swaying. I told that to Rozelle and she got up-tight. She got real scared. She didn't think it was too cool for us to be out in the garage so we went into the house. Well, we had a couple of joints so we lit those and after a while we went out for a walk. That's when things got real freaky. It was out of sight! We went into The Side Pocket, a billiard parlor, and we started to shoot some pool and I looked at the pool balls and I couldn't believe it. The balls started getting ears. Big ears. Like on rabbits. That really broke me up! I mean, I really thought they were rabbits and when I hit one—well, it didn't look like a ball at all, it looked like a rabbit rolling around. Then with its big ears and all it fell in the hole and it was dead. It was really out of sight! I couldn't believe it. I mean—you know, I knew it wasn't rabbits but it sure as hell looked like them. Even though I dug it, I got kind of scared. I started to feel kind of—I don't know, kind of shitty. So I told Rozelle to walk me home and I remember on the way home I said to her, 'I really thought something fantastic was going to happen, but all that happened was the pool balls had rabbit ears.' "

"How did this boy Kenny happen to—by the way, how old was he?"

"Seventeen."

"How did he happen to turn you on to acid?"

"Well, he had turned me on to grass when I was thirteen."

"Oh? Let's start there, then."

"That was when I was in the seventh grade. Actually, I had never smoked at all until that time—not even a cigarette. I mean, I guess like every kid I had taken a couple of puffs but I didn't really smoke, you know. And I remember Kenny got real mad at me because I wouldn't inhale. He said I was wasting it. I tried to inhale once or twice, but it made me sick and dizzy and I just couldn't do it. I didn't smoke pot again for about a year and a half."

"How did you feel about Kenny?"

"I liked him because he was rebellious. He was forever getting into trouble and I thought that was groovy. He always got kicked out of classes or suspended and one time he even got picked up for stealing a car. I remember how that impressed me. And at that time I was such a goody-goody, you couldn't believe it. I was a good student, I was never late for school, I never wore my skirts too short, never wore makeup—I was just a big kiss-ass. I couldn't *stand* myself. I was really a piece of wallpaper and it was a bad scene. Really bad."

"You disliked yourself."

"I hated me. Well, I don't know if I really hated me but I didn't like what I stood for. I mean, nobody knew me because I was so inconspicuous. And I wanted people to know who I was."

"Do people know who you are now?"

"No. People *I* know know who I am, they know my name. But—I don't mean that I wanted to be famous. I just wanted people around me to know who I was. I didn't want to be a part of the wallpaper anymore. And then, remember, I told you that I never had friends when I was young? I was so mean that nobody would have anything to do with me. And after that I became the shy nothing, well—so damn passive."

"Your reaction then, as I understand it—to get over your meanness, you became passive."

"Right. Oh, I was such a kiss-ass. Wow! I used to—you know, the whole bit. The apple on the teacher's desk—all of that shit. I made myself sick. I remember I thought at that time, Boy, wouldn't it be great to be one of the Hell's Angels' women. I mean, everybody knew who they were. But then I saw them and I had to say, 'Forget it.' Wow—you know, I thought it'd be really classy but it's not. It's grubby. And it's dirty."

"Tell me about the boys you dated at that time."

"The first guy I ever really went with was Johnny Foreman. I started going with him when I was fifteen and I went with him for a year and a half. Then he asked me to marry him. He gave me a ring about four months later but I broke our engagement. I decided I didn't really love him because he wasn't a man. I mean, he lived off his parents. Literally. He was twenty-five—no, he was twenty-three—and he was still going to school on his parents' money. Actually I was marrying him to get away from my house. To get away from my father. I really wanted out. So I thought I'd marry him. I even went to bed with him—you know, thinking we were going to get married. No—wait. That's a lie. To be totally honest, I went to bed with him before I ever thought about marrying him."

"Did you go to bed with him because you had a feeling of love at the time or——"

"No. He wanted to, so I did."

"Why?"

"He said if I really loved him, I'd do it. Then I went with Hal Jerome."

"How old was Hal?"

"Twenty-four and he'd been divorced. He was a lush. I don't know if you want to know, but I never went to bed with him."

"Okay. Why not?"

"We just never got around to it. He never tried to touch me, not even one time."

"And you didn't feel inclined to encourage him in any way?"

"Uh-uh. And the entire time we went together I didn't date anyone else. I'm very true when I'm going with a guy. I've never gone out on a guy—not even once. But Hal'd always get up-tight because I wouldn't kiss him. It was really a bad scene. He got mad at me just about every night. Because I wouldn't kiss him."

"Barbara, we've come to a time when we've got to arrive—you've got to arrive at some answers. And they're best arrived at from your subconscious. I'm going to turn on——"

"Please, John! No," Barbara interrupted sharply. "I'd rather just talk. I don't want to be hypnotized."

"I won't insist, but I do think it's important. I wouldn't have suggested it if I didn't think so." Barbara scowled, fidgeted, moved back and forth restlessly in her chair, looked at me steadily for a moment, and then her eyes dropped away. I wasn't to learn yet why she had built up a reluctance to being hypnotized. I didn't say anything, I just waited. After about two minutes—it seemed much longer—Barbara said, "Well, if you think it's necessary."

I reclined Barbara's chair, turned on the flashing lights, and in a matter of moments she was in a sound, deep sleep. Her resistance, obviously, was at a superficial conscious level. I told her to let her mind drift as I counted and at the count of ten she would have a clear understanding of her reluctance to be kissed. When I asked her the reason, she replied, "I don't want to talk about it."

"You have to talk about it. You have to get rid of it, You have to get rid of it from deep inside."

"I know. It's just very hard to say it."

"You have to."

"I knew what my father did with his mouth—where he kissed me. I couldn't get it out of my head. I would always think about it. And after he had his mouth there I couldn't let him kiss me. I guess I felt the same—I know I felt the same about other guys. I didn't know where their mouths had been."

"Fine. That was fine, Barbara. Now let's trace the course of your life from the time that———"

"You mean the intercourse of my life, don't you?" Barbara laughed.

I couldn't help but laugh with her. "Okay, let's trace the intercourse of your life from the first time with———"

"Tony. He was the first one. He was after I broke up with Hal."

"Oh, yes, he was the young man that you and your girlfriend Rozelle and another boy whose name eludes me at this moment—you had double dates and you and Rozelle planned to have sex that night. You took a bath—several baths, in fact—and—"

"Right."

"Now how many different men did you have relations with?"

"Let's see, there was—I told you about Johnny Foreman. Then there was Bruce Michaels, Lee Lawrence, and there was Johnny's uncle, Bernie Foreman, and let's see . . . Henry Galucci, Tom Huston, and Dick Ferguson. I can't remember anybody else right now. If I think of anyone, I'll tell you."

"Okay. That's a deal. And all of those were between the ages of fifteen and seventeen?"

"Right."

"Why did you go to bed with Bruce?"

"Well, like I told you, my family and I are motorcycle nuts. And he'd just gotten this new bike and he took me for a ride. We rode out into the country and it was a beautiful day and—I don't know, we stopped riding and we were out there in the grass—that's funny! We were in the grass smoking grass." Barbara laughed uproariously, and it took several moments before she continued, "And he told me that—you know, that I turned him on. That—well, he told me he had a hard-on. So I told him, 'Okay.' And he just did his little thing."

"What do you mean—he did his little thing?"

"He put it in me and that was it."

"And you didn't get any enjoyment out of it?"

"No way. I remember, he got mad at me. He told me that I was just one step better than masturbating."

"How did that make you feel?"

"I don't remember."

"Barbara, I'm going to count to three. As I count, you are going to go into a deeper sleep and you will remember your feelings after Bruce told you that you were only one step better than masturbation. One—you're going into a deeper sleep. Your mind is going back to that time. Your mind is drifting around that moment and the conversation at that time. Two—you're beginning to realize—beginning to know how you felt when he told you that. Three—tell me your feelings."

"I felt good."

It was like a jigsaw puzzle falling into place. I was delighted by the subconscious admission that she had just made and continued the questioning, "And Lee, tell me about him."

"One time when I had had an argument with Johnny, I went over to Lee's to talk to him about it because Lee was a good friend of mine from school. And we ended up in bed."

"What had you and Johnny argued about?"

"Well, this one night we had a date and he canceled it because he was sick. Later, I saw him out with a girl I knew from school. And I was mad at him for that."

"All right, so you went over to see Lee. Did you have any idea that you might end up in bed with him?"

"No. I don't think so. I didn't think about making love with him or going to bed with him. He was just a friend and I wanted to talk to him, but when I arrived at his house, he was drunk and almost immediately, he told me that he'd always wanted to go to bed with me and I said, 'No, I can't do that, I'm going with Johnny.' And he said, 'Well, he went out on you, didn't he?' And I said, 'Yeah.' And he said, 'Then what's the difference?' Then he told me how much he cared about me and everything like that. I knew it was just a line and I told him, 'No.' And he said, 'Let's just go in the bedroom for a while. I won't do anything, I promise.' So we went in there and he turned on the radio and I had this beautiful green dress on. It wasn't even mine—it was my girlfriend's. Anway, Lee took the dress off me. It was terrible. He just put it in. That was it. He didn't even kiss me."

"Did you want him to?"

"Shit! Anything was better than the way it was."

"Had you tried to stop him?"

"No."

"Did you protest in any way while he was taking off your dress?"

"No."

"Why not?"

"I was very upset about Johnny and Lee had been giving me a line and I guess I wanted to believe it. And you know something? I haven't seen him since. Not once. I've never seen him from that moment to this."

"Okay. I think you said someone named Bernie Foreman, that he was Johnny's uncle—is that right?"

"Yeah. He was Johnny's uncle."

"Johnny was a boy you were going with and you ended up in bed with his uncle—how did that happen?"

"Well, Johnny and I were always fighting and always breaking up every two or three days it seemed. And, well, Bernie wanted to go to bed with me so I did. It seemed I'd always find myself in bed with some other guy. I guess I was just trying to find a substitute, and there wasn't any because they didn't really care, you know. They were just doing their thing. I see it now, but I didn't see it then. That's how I ended up in bed with Tommy Huston."

"Tell me about him."

"He was a hood. I mean a real hood. He was a bastard. He would take his grandmother for her last dime. He really would. One night when I was out with Rozelle and her date—I had just broken up with Johnny about two days before that, and anyway everybody got drunk. I wasn't drinking at all then. I really never did. Anyway, we all went over to Tommy's house and he turned the stereo on and, you know, we broke up into two couples. He had bunk beds in his bedroom. And Rozelle and her date got in the top bunk and me and him in the bottom and he started all this shit and, honestly, I didn't even try to resist. And after he balled me—wow! Did he ever get mad."

"Again, because you were passive during intercourse?"

"Yes."

"Now, Barbara, think carefully. Think very carefully and don't answer me right away. Do you think you enjoyed letting them have sex with you, but frustrating them because they didn't satisfy you? Did you enjoy that?"

Barbara was silent for many moments then answered, "Yes—that was it. I really put them down and it made me feel good to do it. It made me feel happy. It gave me a kick to put a guy down—that way, I mean. Not with words, or not going out with them, or standing them up, but that way. Because it really got to them. It really did."

"How did you learn about putting men down this way?"

"Because of my father."

"Tell me about it."

"Any time my dad would get mad and—you know, get mad at me, I'd do something like that and it'd really piss him off. It would make him furious."

"That's how you got back at him."

"Yes."

"So you'd just be dead—passive."

"I couldn't have cared less. I could have read a magazine while he was doing it to me."

"And how would he react to that?"

"He'd be furious. Absolutely up-tight—just wow!"

"And you used this same attitude, this passiveness, with everybody that you went to bed with, didn't you?"

"Yes, it really pissed them off. And it made me glad. It made me very glad."

I relaxed. Therapy was going exceedingly well. What Barbara had just said was the blueprint for a nymphomaniac.

Tenth Visit,

JANUARY 13

"When will I be able to read everything I've said?"

"I'm having the tapes transcribed. When they're ready and when I think you're ready to read them, I'll give them to you. It shouldn't be too much longer. How are you feeling?"

"Great. Better than I've felt in years. Really. I haven't been this happy in a long time."

"Did anything happen these past weeks that you think I should know about?"

"Well, maybe a couple of things. My mom called and I got to talk to her and Holly. And after I hung up, I got a terrible headache. It was weird."

"Oh?"

"Maybe it was because our relationships were always so difficult."

"Yours and your mother's?"

"That, and mine and Holly's. I mean I was always going to kill Holly—constantly. Maybe not consciously, but once she passed out from what I did. There was always this terrible conflict between us."

"Do you recall what caused this?"

"I was jealous. I thought she might get close to my dad."

"Then you did worry about that?"

"I don't know if I worried about it consciously then but I know now, that's what it was."

"You are consciously aware that you were afraid Holly would get close to your dad?"

"Right."

"That's worth tonight's entire session! Good work, Barbara! Now tell me, was there any suggestion that your dad could get as close to her as he was with you?"

"No, but I think dad was the only thing I had to hold on to. He was the only thing that was really mine. And I didn't want *any*body to be messing around with that. Especially not Holly because I had to fight my mom as it was. I was smart enough to realize that two people were going to make it twice as hard. And besides, I was jealous of her getting close to my brothers."

"Why was that?"

"They were mine, too, in the sense that we were closer in age than Holly. And I didn't want her taking any of the attention away from me."

Insights and admissions on a completely conscious level had begun and therapy was moving ahead much more quickly than even I had anticipated. "How are things going between you and Walter?"

"I'm not living there anymore. I moved out."

"Oh? What happened?"

"It just wasn't a good scene anymore. I mean, when I came in there everything was, 'I love you' and all of that shit. Now he starts in about my going out to look for a job. That's how bad it got. He'd say, 'Money is going to stop. You need a job. Go out and get one.' And I'd say, 'I won't.' And he'd say, 'You can't keep living off of me.' And well—it was a bad scene."

"Where are you living?"

"I'm sleeping on the couch at Charles' family."

"Who is Charles?"

"Charles? He's this guy I met at Scientology. Heh, that's right, I never did tell you how when I was living with Walter and Sandy, they never got mad or anything. Never even raised their voices. It was groovy. It was so beautiful I just had to know why. What made it like that? They told me it was Scientology. They were members of Scientology and so I went to a lecture with them. It was a very, very good lecture. I mean, in the beginning I didn't believe anything they said, I thought it was all a bunch of shit. When I argued with them they said, 'Why don't you get a couple of bulletins and read them and then see what you have to say?' Well, I read the bulletins and I dug what they said. So I've been out there at Scientology and that's where I met Charles. When I moved out of Walter's I didn't have any place to go so Charles asked his mom if it was okay for me to sleep on the sofa. And really, John, nothing is going on between me and Charles. Honest. And you know what? Charles and another guy, Carlos, and a girl, Julie, and I are going to go to Oahu and open a franchise there. A Scientology franchise. I'm really grooving on it. It's out of sight. It's like nothing else I have ever known."

"We'll get back to this in a moment but before I forget, because I've been meaning to ask, what's with you and drugs?"

"Nothing. The last time I dropped acid was back in Farrell before I came down to L. A. and I haven't smoked pot in—it's about two weeks now. And I've never made the uppers or downers scene. I just didn't dig that. And I'm even off birth control pills."

"*Those* you can take," I said laughing.

"There's no reason for me to take them, John. I'm not doing anything now to need them."

"That's most interesting. You mean you've had a change in your sexual drive?"

"Well, I've begun to realize that I didn't really want it and they didn't really want me—they were just after sex. So I just don't see any point in it anymore. And I've stopped. And like over at Charles' house last night, we were doing our TRs, and TRs are just being— acknowledging the fact that you are there and somebody else is there. You're not trying to be interesting or happy or funny or sad or anything—you know, you're just there. Anyhow, we were listening to music and then we started laughing. And it was funny because you reach a point where you're totally relaxed and nothing's on your mind and you're not worried or upset or anything. We just laughed because it was groovy. I don't know if you know anything about Scientology, but they have what they call the 'eight dynamics' and the first dynamic is survival through self. The second is survival through sex and the rearing of children. Scientology doesn't have anything against sex. They don't say do it or they don't say don't do it. Because Scientology is totally an individual thing. It's like—okay, it's your bag. And because like nobody is saying to me, don't have sex—I don't see any point in having it. And I think, John, I used to have sex with the guys because it made me important. But now I find that I'm important just by myself. I mean like, shit, I'm having a groovy time now and I'm not doing anything but being me. Just me. And it's groovy. Especially because I don't even have to lie anymore."

"You accept yourself."

"Right."

"That's marvelous."

"Yeah."

"How do you feel about Bob now?"

"Bob? Okay. That's a part of my life that's over with."

"Good. I don't know if you recall but during one of our first interviews you felt that you'd never be able to accept his being gone. But you have accepted it."

"Yes."

"John," Barbara continued, "I have something to tell you. All of a sudden this past week things have begun to pop into my mind. A lot of things— And one thing has been bothering me. There's something I've lied about and I think I should tell you."

"What's that?"

"I think I told you that I didn't go to bed with Paul Jackson. The boy that stayed with me when I was sick."

"Oh, yes. That's right—that's what you told me."

"Well, I did."

A CASE HISTORY OF INCEST

"Okay. You did."

"You're not mad at me for lying to you?"

"No. Do you feel better now that you've told me?"

"Yes. A lot better."

"Good. Now, Barbara, there's one thing in particular and I'd like you to try to follow carefully what I'm saying. In your nightmares—your dreams, and, in fact, in your daily living—you've had fears of hanging. Many of your death-oriented thoughts have had to do with decapitation and hanging."

"Yes."

"Even when you've gotten angry, as you've told me, with your sister you tried to strangle her—again having to do with the head or neck. Do you know why?"

"No."

"Try to think of someone decapitated—do you remember anyone that way?"

"No. Just when I was a kid, in Formosa, and I saw the skulls on top of graves."

"Besides that. Did you ever visualize or see anyone with his head off?"

"Uh-uh."

"How about your dad?"

"My dad? With his head off?"

"Think about it. When he was having sexual relations with you—think of the positions your bodies were in. His position in relationship to you. Your mind was active—you've told me. You thought of many things. I assume your eyes were open and you may have looked at your dad. Now, from the position you were in and your dad was in—if you...."

"I couldn't see his head!"

A look of complete amazement spread slowly across Barbara's face. "Wow! That's out of sight! You're right, John! I could only see him up to here—" and Barbara drew a line across her neck.

"Well, we got that cleared up."

"You mean all of my nightmares and fears of hanging, all have to do with that?"

"I believe so."

"Wow!"

"It shows how angry you were with your father. Now, and I want you to think about this: You used to tend to be more sexually aroused by individuals that you didn't care too much for as persons, and—you're shaking your head 'yes.' "

"Uh-huh."

"Do you know why?"

"Because of my father. Because I liked him as a person and I had sex with him, and he hurt me. Does that make sense? I mean, if I didn't care about a person, then they couldn't care about me either and that way they couldn't hurt me, through sex. But a person I cared about, if I had sex with them and they turned me away, it might crush me. So, it was better to have sex with people. I didn't care for. That way I could feel freer. Right?"

"I couldn't have done a better job explaining it myself. Now there's another area that I only touched on briefly, under hypnosis. And that's your father's attempt to have intercourse with you. I believe, from what you've told me, it was when you were eight."

"Well, that was the first time. And he kept trying through the years but it was never consummated. Of course, when he first tried it, I didn't even realize what it was—not until they started teaching about it in school. Then I didn't understand how anyone could get pleasure out of it. It sounded absolutely repulsive. I didn't actually understand what it meant. I mean, I knew that my dad was trying to do it, but I didn't know what it was, if that makes sense. What I mean is, if somebody said that he was trying to screw me, I would have said that he wasn't. That's not what it's like."

"How would he approach trying to have intercourse with you?"

"First he would go down on me. Then he'd start messing around with my chest. Then he would pull himself up and say you know—he'd look at me like 'please?' and I'd say that it hurt. Or I'd just say no, or I'd start crying and then he'd get mad or he wouldn't get mad, depending on what he decided to do. If he got mad, he'd push me away and I'd try to apologize but that generally didn't do any good, so I'd get up and leave or go into my bedroom and cry. Then, later when I'd come out, he'd say that he was sorry, that he really wasn't angry with me."

"Did he make these attempts frequently?"

"Not too often. Maybe once every three months. Mostly it was just going down on me. And me—sometimes, going down on him. I mean, I didn't go down on him every time he went down on me."

"And his attempts at intercourse were always the same.

"Well, yes, that is—all except one time."

"Tell me about that."

"Well, I think I was—it was past my thirteenth birthday, and mom had taken my brothers and Holly fishing for the weekend. Dad and I were going to stay home because he had to work and I was to keep him company. Anyway, when he came home from work on Friday, he got me drunk. Then we played the game and after we'd played the game for a while, he told me to get on my hands and knees and he tried to have intercourse. You know—I guess they call it 'dog-fashion.' Anyway, by then we'd been boozing for about four hours and I was so drunk that every time he pushed against me, I fell flat on my face. Once he almost managed to enter me, but I fell again. Wow, did he get mad! It really put him on a bummer."

"Was that the only time he ever attempted to get you drunk?"

"Yeah. I guess he figured it didn't work out too well the one time he tried it."

"Did you ever enjoy having oral relations with him?"

"No. I mean—in the very beginning I can remember him saying, 'Okay, now you do it.' And I'd say, 'Do what?' And he'd push my head down—you know, down to his thing, and I'd look at him like he was crazy.

Then he'd tell me what to do and I'd do it a little. Then I'd stop."

"Have you ever gotten to enjoy an oral relationship?"

"Yes. The first time was with Bob."

"You had never practiced fellatio on any other man—other than your dad—until you got married?"

"Uh-huh—that's right."

"You did enjoy it with Bob?"

"Yes. I mean, he didn't ask me. I just did it."

"Now you were seventeen and a half when you married Bob. Did he ask you where you learned or heard about fellatio?"

"Well, he knew about me and my dad and I guess he just figured I had learned it there."

"And you have practiced this with men since you broke up with Bob?"

"Oh, yes, I really dig on it!"

"Are you still continuing to experience orgasms?"

"Yes. Definitely."

"Can you attempt to describe an orgasm?"

"Well, I don't know, but I'll try. Before, sort of building up to it, you know?—it's sort of a pleasant turmoil. Kind of a warm feeling that starts in my fingertips and toes and then spreads until I feel very warm all over, like it's a summer's day. Not hot, just warm, completely warm and comfortable. It's groovy. Then, there's kind of an explosion and I want to scream. My fingernails are sharp and I have to be careful because I found out I scratch."

"Do you still have a desire to become pregnant?"

"I think there would be nothing greater, but I know it would be wrong—completely unthinkable at this time."

"I agree with that. Do you know the significance of your wanting to become pregnant?"

"Not completely."

"In many respects, your relationships to people are a desire to possess them. For example, possessing your brothers, your father, even your mother and your sister. You always try to possess the people around you.

And the desire for a child is a continuation of that feeling. You want a child to possess."

". . . hearing you say it, it makes sense to me. But I know it'd be stupid to have a child now. I may be a lot of things but I'm not stupid."

"One parting question—your relationship with Allan and Ronnie," I began, and watched Barbara as she reacted, curiosity written across her face. "Do you think you could enter into that type of relationship again?"

"I told you about that, huh?—I guess I must have. No, John, I could never do that again. It was ugly. Just ugly."

This was the first time, since our very first meeting, that I did not have to awaken Barbara from a hypnotic sleep and erase the memory of the session with her. We had come a long way and I felt she was ready to read the transcriptions of all of our recorded interviews. Read about her life as she had described it from a subconscious level: the contradictions and turmoil and all the machinations that were caused by an incestuous relationship; the misconceptions of love and hate, and how these were interlaced—and often mistaken each for the other. As she had said, some of the information had drifted from her subconscious to her conscious mind in the past week. Her conscious mind could now accept some of the horrors from her subconscious because Barbara had come to accept herself. In accepting herself, she could accept those things—those actions from the past. If she had not been able to do this, none of the material from our sessions could have made its way into her conscious mind.

I told Barbara that I would have to call her to set the time for our next appointment as I did not know how long it would take to have the tapes transcribed. She paled a little and her eyes opened wide, "You mean— John, you mean that I'm ready—you think I'm ready to read it?"

Eleventh Visit,

JANUARY 24

My first appointment was scheduled for 8 A.M. and I had called Barbara and asked her if it were possible for her to be at my office at seven-thirty. The tapes had been transcribed into six hundred pages of typewritten material. It would take her hours to read them and I wanted to be nearby, in case the material had a traumatic effect on her.

I gave Barbara the pages at ten minutes of eight and left her in the office adjoining mine. I saw little of her during the day. Once, around eleven, she asked for the key to the ladies' room and at twelve-thirty I brought her a hamburger, French fries, and a coke. I took her out to a nearby restaurant at six-fifteen and throughout dinner she was strangely silent. She returned to the room and closeted herself with the pages again until nine-twenty. After a coffee break we sat down to discuss everything she had read.

Although Barbara had told me that a lot of what had been said under hypnoisis had drifted into her conscious mind, I did not realize to what extent this had taken place. And it, of course, dispelled the traumatic effect I thought reading the material might have had.

Barbara thumbed through the pages and we discussed many aspects of her relationships. She seemed particularly disturbed about the number of men with whom she had gone to bed. She said, "Until I saw it in print, I had no idea it had been that many."

"Do you know what nymphomania means?"

"Yes," Barbara answered in a subdued voice.

"Would you consider yourself a nymphomaniac?"

Barbara hesitated a long time before answering. Then after several starts, she said, "Not really. From what I understand about the word, I would say no."

I pursued, "What does the word mean?"

"It's someone who enjoys sex but can't ever be satisfied."

"Not necessarily, Barbara," I said. "Ordinarily a nymphomaniac doesn't enjoy it. She does not have a climax."

"John—" Barbara began, "John, please don't tell me that, okay?"

"Does that frighten you?" I asked.

"That's what Tina, my father's first wife, was. And I've always said that I may be just like her, but in that one thing—I wasn't. John, that would really hurt. Don't tell me that."

"That reminds me of—do you ever watch 'Get Smart'?"

"Uh-huh."

"Well, in the show, Maxwell Smart says, 'Don't tell me that,' and his adversary says it and he says, 'I told you not to tell me.'"

"I—I already knew it," Barbara mumbled. "I just didn't want to hear anybody say it."

"Barbara, listen to me. No, no, don't look away. If you are a nymphomaniac and you don't like it, you can stop it. Or, if you are, and you don't want to be, but you don't want to stop—you have to learn to accept it. What you're doing right now is the worst thing you can do—feeling guilty about it, and trying to deny it to yourself. But you're not hiding it, you see, it's still there. You're not stupid. In fact, you're very bright. And part of your brain knows exactly what you're doing."

"All of it knows."

"Okay, perhaps there is a semantic difference between promiscuousness and nymphomania. I'm not sure there is, but—what is your mind doing right now?"

"Doing its best to accept what's been said. It's not easy."

"Do you disapprove of it?"

"Yes, I do. Because Tina's life was one big fucked-up mess. I don't want mine to be that way. All my life I've been told 'You're just like Tina. You look like Tina. You talk and think like Tina. You're Tina.' "

"Who told you that?"

"My dad."

"Is the reason, then, that you don't want to be a nymphomaniac that your father always talked disparagingly about Tina?"

"No. My dad never put her down for that. He didn't like her sleeping around when they were married but—it's just that I don't want to be anybody else. And that very thing makes me her. That was the only thing that made me not her—and now, suddenly, I'm her."

"No. You're not Tina ,you're just a nympho. Let me put it this way, Barbara—you exhibit the behavior. At least until recently."

"Well, I don't think I'm a nympho in the real sense. I think I am in the sense that I need affection and, even though it's false, the feeling that someone cares about me is what I'm after, and if I have to go to bed with them to get that feeling, I do it. But as far as enjoying it or even wanting it, I don't."

"In other words—you're willing to give somebody sex in order to buy affection."

"Right."

"Okay. What would you call that?"

"A whore. Okay?" Barbara hurled the words at me.

"You're making the definitions."

"My definition is, I'm just somebody who's very—I dig on affection and. . . ."

"Has anyone ever given you real affection in trade for sex?"

"Yes. Bob. When we were married."

"Real affection?"

"Well, yes, before the shit started flying." Then Barbara interjected, "You mean, John, that I get punishment for something that I didn't do because nobody is born to be a nymphomaniac?"

"How do you mean, punished?"

"With this feeling, this urge through my entire life."

"How does being a nymphomaniac punish you?"

"It plays hell with ever having any security."

"Right!"

"I'm pretty smart," Barbara said triumphantly.

"Yes, but does that make you a bad person?"

"No."

"Are you a bad person?"

"No."

"Have you ever been?"

"No. Not with intention."

"Barbara, do you want to stop being a nympho?"

"Do I want to stop? If you're going to put me under hypnosis to do it, no. If you can do it consciously, okay."

"I'm not going to do it at all. You're going to have to do it if you want to stop."

"I see. Okay. I think I can do it myself. In fact, I was thinking about it just last night. Last night I said, 'Okay, Barbara, if you're going to do it, at least pick one guy. You don't need every other guy around and it's not going to do you any good.' And, John, Walter loves me. I'm not saying I love him—I guess I do in a way. I mean, I wouldn't marry him right now. I might later, but even though I moved out of his place, we're dating. And it's groovy—real boy-girl stuff. You know what I mean? But I decided, No more screwing around. No more. You know, I used to lie in bed at night and say to myself, 'You're a nympho! You're a nympho! You're a nympho!' And I didn't believe it. I knew it, but I wouldn't accept it. It's like somebody with cancer—knowing they have cancer, a terminal case of it, and not believing that they're going to die. It's just like that. I knew I was a nympho. I've known it for a long time but I couldn't accept it. And you know what else?"

"No," I said.

"I don't think I've told a lie in the last week. I've stopped lying. I can't believe it," Barbara said animatedly.

"Are you lying now?"

"No," Barbara laughed. Then she went on, "John—I talked to my folks this past week and, of course, they asked how I was getting along. I told them fine, that I thought that we had made a lot of progress. And, then—well, my dad said that he'd like to talk to you. That there were two sides to everything and mother and he would like to give you theirs. I told them I'd tell you that I talked to them and, I don't know—I guess you could call, if you wanted to."

It was too late to call them that night and I told Barbara I would call the following day. I looked at her for a moment and then said, "Barbara, important point—do you recognize that your lack of having a climax is an expression of hostility?"

"Yes, definitely. But there's not the slightest doubt that I have climaxes with Walter. He's the only one that I would seek out, no matter where he was, because he's the only one that has ever satisfied me."

"What about Webb?"

"No. Not really."

"I thought he had satisfied you? That you had experienced an orgasm with him."

"Well, then I did. But, after Walter—I mean, now I know what it is to really have an orgasm. I mean, it's really great with Walter. He's not aggressive and he's not passive. And I'm not aggressive and I'm not passive. It's like we work together—it's really groovy."

"Fine. And how about your dreams? Are you still dreaming?"

"Just about every night."

"What sort of dreams?"

"Happy ones. Groovy dreams. But one strange

thing, I keep dreaming about people running out of gas and me giving them money to buy some."

"Do you think the dreams have a relationship to something specific?"

"I don't know. The other night I hitchhiked to Venice and I got picked up by these two guys who could hardly speak English. And when I got out—they weren't going all the way out to Venice, you know—so they gave me a dollar for the bus. It was so sweet of them, yet when I got out of the car I tried to think of them as suckers. I sat down on the bus stop and I was thinking that, then I realized it was dumb. I mean, I tried to think bad of them, which was dumb—but I couldn't really do it—that is, think of them as suckers."

"Why would you try to think of them as suckers?"

"That would have been my normal attitude and I would have thought that way, even up to last month. I mean, I know I would have thought they were suckers then. But, sitting there on the bus stop, I realized they were just nice guys."

I was delighted. As a psychopath she would have thought of them only as suckers. Her attitude now was much more normal. I continued, "Barbara, money is an area that I've been meaning to talk to you about. That is your ability to get money out of people."

"Everybody down at Scientology wants to know how I do it. I honestly wish I didn't know how to do it sometimes."

"You don't really."

"I guess not but, John, for real, I don't do it on purpose. Everybody I meet goes, 'You're such a nice kid. Is there anything I can do for you?' And I can't say no because I need a lot of things."

"That isn't entirely true. You've had plenty of money to buy food but you've given it away."

"Yeah, but they usually needed it more than I do."

"But how does that affect your life?"

"It screws it up because I give my money away. If I had all the money I gave away, I'd be rich."

"What are you trying to do by giving your money away?"

"Repent."

"Aha! Repent for what?"

"For all the things I've done wrong. All the shit that I've pulled on everybody."

"It's not to buy affection?"

"No. Because the people I give my money to—I mean, I just dig on giving things away. And I've always seemed able to get money when no one else could. And I figure those other people are in worse predicaments than I'm in. I mean, they're hungry and can't get money out of other people. And I'm hungry and I've got money so I can give them the money for their hunger and I can go get other money for mine. If that makes sense."

"Is it possible that you're testing whether or not people care for you by trying to get things out of them?"

"No, because I'd rather take something from somebody I didn't know."

"But you do realize that you're taking advantage of somebody, either in your mind by calling them a sucker or—that it's a hostile gesture."

"I never thought about it that way, John, but I see your point. I not only see it, I have to agree—you're right."

"Now, Barbara, and I want you to think about this, what is the most satisfying aspect of the material you've read?"

"I don't have to think about that, John. It's when I quit talking about Cindy and started talking about me."

"Exactly. If you can describe it to me, how did you feel when you read that?"

"I accepted, for the first time, that it was me. It wasn't anybody else—it was me. It was a great relief and yet it was a lot of pain. It gave me a headache. Just reading it, I got a severe headache. After that though, everything came pretty easily. But before that it was very, very difficult. I don't know if this makes sense, but I felt good when I realized who I was. And what I was."

"Fine. That's very good. Can you tell me what you found in terms of who you were—or who you are?"

"Yes. I feel I was a very mixed-up girl who was put into some circumstances that were very difficult. In my opinion, for whatever it's worth, I came out pretty well considering everything. I think I'm a nice person basically. I may be a little stingy, but I'm nice. I have my faults but I have my good points, too. Except, I was pretty hung up on my faults. Almost to the point where the only things I had were faults."

"You're seeing yourself as a confused girl who was all involved in her own faults. But now, all of a sudden, you can see that you do have some good points."

"Yes."

"And how does that make you feel?"

"Great. Just great—I feel that I know me. And that really, I'm kind of groovy."

"I think you are, too."

The next day I called and talked with Barbara's father and mother in Farrell. The following facts were discovered through that conversation.

Henry Gale described the years of his marriage to Tina as an agonizing experience during which time she slept with some thirty different men. He recalled at one point walking down a street on the base and meeting his wife with a chief petty officer he knew only slightly. When he approached them and asked, "What the hell are you doing with my wife?" the man replied, "Shit, Hank, if I'd known she was your wife, I never would have banged her."

Gale also related that Tina took great pleasure in making him sit and listen to her describe her love trysts in detail before she would resume any relationship with him.

After two years of this torturous existence Gale sued for divorce.

Soon after the divorce became final, he met Geraldine, his present wife, Barbara's mother. She was the complete opposite of Tina. She had never dated a boy before going out with Seaman Gale. They married after a short courtship and, within two months, he was reassigned to Corpus Christi, Texas.

Five months after their marriage, the new Mrs. Gale became pregnant and the prospective parents were delighted. In June of that year, when she was in her sixth month, he was assigned to sea duty and did not return until their first child, a boy, Stuart, was four months old. Because of this separation, during the last three months of the pregnancy and the first four months of his son's life, Gale said he has never felt close to his son.

He was distraught to learn, on his return, that the doctors had informed Mrs. Gale that she was Rh negative and she'd been very fortunate that there hadn't been any complications during the birth and also that the child had not been deformed. They were advised by the doctor not to have any more children as each succeeding birth would multiply the danger to her life during delivery and/or increase the likelihood of deformity in the child.

Eight months later, when Mrs. Gale found she was pregnant again, they applied to the Navy doctors for a therapeutic abortion, but this was denied.

However, having been forewarned that the risk of death increased with each conception, the Gales entered into nine months of abject fear. As her delivery date grew closer and closer, Mrs. Gale became terrified at the thought that she might die.

In December of 1950, their second child, Barbara, was born. Barbara was not deformed and Mrs. Gale survived. However, the nine months of anguish, fear, and terror through which the Gales lived, somehow had their effect on Barbara. The infant, only four pounds and three ounces at birth, could not hold down any food. At the same time she developed a case of severe diarrhea. Both of these conditions persisted for the first eight months of Barbara's life. Doctors, both on the

A CASE HISTORY OF INCEST

base and in Corpus Christi, told the Gales not to expect their daughter to live—that Barbara might last a few weeks or perhaps only a few days. Somehow, however, this frail infant managed to hold onto life by a thread. This thread was so slight that several times during these eight months the Gales were forced to leave Barbara in the hospital so she could be fed intravenously. Her condition was listed as "critical" for days and weeks at a time.

Because of the hardships involved in keeping their child comfortable, the Gales had taken to constantly holding Barbara across their laps and patting her to sleep. They soon found this was the only way they could keep her comfortable, and so perhaps twenty out of every twenty-four hours would find either parent holding the infant.

An obvious natural resentment began to grow in them, and they admitted that many times during those months they silently wished Barbara would die. This caused great guilt feelings, which were further magnified by a marine and his wife who lived in adjoining barracks. They had a sickly child, too, and one day when Barbara was about five months old, Mrs. Gale went out to put out her wash and found they had hung their baby by the neck from the clothesline.

When Barbara reached nine months of age, she suddenly began to keep down food and lead a more normal existence, and life became less of a physical and emotional strain for her parents. Then about a year later, Mrs. Gale found herself pregnant, and the terror and fear started again. At this time the Gales discontinued sexual intercourse and began an oral-genital relationship.

It was here that I got to the root of my feeling of error when I told Barbara her head felt so big because she was only three years old.* The head of a three-year-old child as compared to an adult's, is proportionately bigger than his body, but I had a feeling it

*See page 29.

was not that much bigger. When both the parents described what had transpired during her illness, it became clear that Barbara in her hypnosis, had been regressed back to less than six *months* old, and at this age the infant's head *is* distinctly proportionately larger. The interpretation was correct, but Barbara had been regressed considerably further back than I had suspected.

Their third child was born, and once again, the infant was unscarred and Mrs. Gale suffered no ill effects, beating all the mathematical odds against cases with Rh negative blood. They stated that the only other time they engaged in sexual intercourse was some two years later when Mrs. Gale conceived their fourth and last child. It was at this time, when Barbara was three years old, that Mr. Gale began molesting her.

In discussing this relationship with me, he said, "If you were to tell me that I would do anything like that to my child, I would tell you you were crazy. Yet, I know I did it. I hated myself for it. But I found I couldn't stop myself."

Mrs. Gale said, "While I was never sure what was going on, I did feel there was something wrong with Henry spending so much time with Barbara. It got so Barbara was the lady of the house. By the time she was seven, she was literally running the house, telling me what to do, telling me what to fix for dinner, and what the whole family was going to do on the weekends. Even with the other children—I'd tell them they couldn't go to the park, or some place, and then, moments later, I'd find them leaving; and they'd tell me Barbara had said it was all right for them to go. Ever since she was a little girl, I didn't feel Barbara was my daughter, I felt she was my rival."

CONCLUSION

Barbara had come a long way since our initial meeting. How far can be seen from the following brief recapitulation of what transpired in therapy.

The first interview was simply a fishing trip on my part: What was the problem? What were its main elements in terms of family background, present situation, and other factors? How did she feel about it? What had she done or planned to do about it? The purpose was to obtain an overall picture to help me evaluate Barbara's capacity to gain insight and to test her motivation for finding a solution. Initially, I was doubtful about her wish to be helped. This, plus her psychopathic personality, did not augur well for a cure. The only hope was in allowing her own depression to intensify to such an extent that it would become a self-propelling force.

I saw the first possibility for a cure when Barbara cried so profusely during the first hypnotic session. This behavior was honest. Even though she did not always tell the truth, her tears indicated that she possessed the kind of emotions upon which human relationships are founded. Even though she was not completely accurate, she wasn't really lying. Her denial that incest was a problem is an example. To her conscious mind her relationship with her father was not a problem. However it *was* a problem to her unconscious mind and it required the deepest, most extensive hypnotic trance for Barbara to come to grips with it. From the point where she denied that she had a problem to the admission that she feared she was lying represented tremendous progress, not only because the unconscious was opening up, indicating increased contact with reality but because a conscience was beginning to take shape. Contact with reality and a conscience are necessary prerequisites for the transformation of a psychopath into a normal person.

Barbara's unconscious conflicts revealed themselves on numerous occasions, as for example her denial of a feeling in one breath, then its confirmation in the next on page 26, where she said, "I've been pretty shitty all my life." As this statement does not reflect self-admiration, I suggested, "Perhaps you hate yourself." The reply was, "No, I don't hate myself, I am only disappointed in me," which was considerably less intense. A moment later she said, "Oh, if you knew all the horrid, horrid things I've done," which again betrayed a very strong emotion and accurately confirmed my initial interpretation of self-hate that was to be amply demonstrated in subsequent sessions. Contradictions like these should not be interpreted as lying. They represent the door of the unconscious being forced open against nearly insurmountable counterpressures to keep it closed. When this became evident I placed Barbara under deeper hypnosis to help relieve the pressure.

The "horrid, horrid thing" referred to on page 26, was the blackmail of her father, which was exposed in therapy. She loved her father as a lover and enjoyed being sexually stimulated by him, but this was buried so deep in her unconscious that it was not revealed to her conscious mind until much later. Up to that time she had never been able to recognize and assuage, in its entirety, the horrible guilt she felt in the eyes of her God.

I would like to reiterate that the inaccuracies in Barbara's accounts were invaluable because they were indicative of unconscious sources of conflict.

It became apparent, during the first hypnotic session, how Barbara's psychopathic personality had developed.

A CASE HISTORY OF INCEST

The psychopath is a manipulator; he uses others, frequently in a socially unacceptable manner, to gain his own ends. Barbara's father taught her how to manipulate by placing himself in a position to be blackmailed. And because her respect for her mother and father was destroyed by their behavior, she also rejected their value system, the good with the bad.

I struck upon the use of Cindy spontaneously (see page 32). It proved so successful a technique that I have employed it in several successive cases with equally satisfactory results.

The guilt from the pleasure she experienced in the sexual relationship with her father can be roughly compared to what happened to Adam after he partook of fruit from the tree of knowledge. As Barbara said, "Cindy was really a nice little girl" (page 34.) When she lost her innocence she tried to hide. But in her soul she could no more conceal her guilt than Adam or Eve. In her mind, the wrath of God was an ever-present spectre.

A glimmer of her homosexual conflict came out and was reflected in her tendency to interchange such words as "guy and girl." Her homosexual problem, of course, resulted from her conflicting feelings about her mother. She hated her mother, yet strove to win her love. In her immature mind, she concluded that if her father's love could be maintained by providing him with sexual pleasures, perhaps her mother's love could be won in the same fashion. Again (see page 173) she took pride in having two lesbians indulging her by selling the *Free Press*. Here she unconsciously fulfilled her homosexual fantasies toward her mother, although consciously she rejected it. The slow, tortuous revelation about her feelings toward homosexuality was one of the more significant keys to Barbara's cure.

Cindy also brought out Barbara's feelings toward Holly (see page 40) whom she wanted to kill for fear that her father would shift his attention to her. This jealousy, too, was deeply traumatic and could not be faced until the end of treatment.

Fear of her father loving Holly was stimulated by finding her father engaged in cunnilingus with her mother. She became jealous of her mother, then of her sister, then of everyone—even me. This was demonstrated (see page 40) when the telephone rang and I had to leave her to answer it. Her whole body began to shake, tremble, and twist violently. This episode, in turn, triggered off associations about her mother and father. Her jealousy even extended to my unknown caller and she punished me by refusing to let Cindy talk any more. I don't believe I have ever experienced a more fruitful interview than this one during my entire twenty years of practice.

More valuable information was gained through analysis of her LSD trips. In the first trip (page 44), she saw herself as an "open book." ". . . you could read the printing across my face and words were written down my body like a book." This image was generated by feelings of guilt arising from the thought that others knew about her incestuous relations with her father. Her reference to "shafts of wheat" reflected her concern with fertility, which in turn manifested itself in her desire to become pregnant. But pregnant by whom? She was suffering guilt (open book) because she wanted to become pregnant by her father but feared she was committing a mortal sin for having such thoughts and, therefore, would be consigned to eternal damnation (fire and hell). This was the first clue to the depth of her religious feeling and the terrible fear she experienced as a result of the way she loved her father and her secret desires for him.

Fire also symbolized a cleansing agent. Whenever she became pregnant, or desired to—such as with her father—she was purified by flames. In this LSD trip her rebirth was signified by the ancient instruments of fertility—the hoes and the rakes—instruments designed to make things grow. The "guy" in the bathtub is also "clean." The darkness and candles (phallic symbols) represented intercourse that culminated in a grand and glorious climax (the bright, flashing colors) without

A CASE HISTORY OF INCEST

LSD (without guilt). It was most beautiful for her. Now she "could tell you anything" (no secrets). But then she returned to reality. She was "busted" by the police, for she still loved her father.

The most important aspect of this acid-dream were the religious connotations. The symbolism was rich and extensive. It imparted exactly what she felt must occur within the rites of purification—at least symbolically—before she could be cured. After reliving this acid-dream, she could freely, frankly, and in full detail, describe her sexual encounters with her father. And she related them as Barbara, not Cindy. She also began gaining further insight into the type of love she had for her father (page 50) and the mixed feelings it produced in her. Her feelings about seeing her father in the act of cunnilingus and its relationship to her reaction to kissing also began here. Here, too, I heard the first reference to the "animal look." Though I did not interpret the meaning of the acid-dream, Barbara's unconscious understood that through catharsis the purging of her mind and her soul had begun.

Her reaction to having actual sexual intercourse with her father, however, was still a highly sensitive point because of its relationship to impregnation. Cunnilingus was a game (at least until the father exhibited the animalistic release of a climax), but intercourse was a sin. Intercourse also represented a complete displacement of the mother. And although Barbara competed with her mother, she never wanted to actually destroy her. She needed her mother's love and there was always a faint hope that her mother would respond. This was so poignantly portrayed (see page 60) when Barbara, after her terrible beating, crawled to her mother's bed. She so longed for her mother's love that even the smell of her in the bedding was comforting.

Previous interviews had yielded copious data. In this interview transference began, and as a consequence, her conscience began to develop.

Yet she resisted me (page 69) as I probed deeper and deeper into her unconscious. Her bad acid trip was particularly revealing. Again, the rich guilt-laden religious symbolism. In this trip, death was the prevalent motif. Death was the dryness. Death was the wilting trees and flowers. Death was her relationship to Sharon and Frank who represented her mother and father. She stole Frank (father) from Sharon (mother.) They were to be married. At first she was ecstatic but confusion of sexual identity ("we're dressed alike") developed. She felt guilt and feared dying herself—"she is beginning to dry out." While Sharon (mother) was away, she and Frank took advantage of her absence, as she and her father had done when daddy took her to mommy's bed (page 64). She could not enjoy it (bum acid), nor have a climax. The damp ground reminded her of the damp ground under the box in Formosa where she taught the other children the games. Also the graveyard was symbolic of guilt and death because of her relationship to her father and her sex play with the children. Her guilt (the guard) was shown even though she was not caught. Again, sex was all right—"we'll make a game of it, like tag"—but not if father (Frank) was in earnest. The "pale, see-through, ghostlike blue" represented the soul and deep within her soul she rejected Frank (father) in the role of lover. She was terrified. Frank was divided into two parts. One was love and life; the other, sex and death. People's bodies were divided between love-life and sex-death. The cop (punishment) returned and the funeral parlor (death) appeared.

Sharon (mother) gave Barbara the bum acid (the sour mother's milk, representing rejection). Sharon made positive approaches to Barbara but her approach is cold. Finally the significant conflict was revealed when Barbara said of Sharon, "I hate her. I don't—I've never said I hated her before." And then (see page 71) she said, "I don't really hate her. I just hate things she does." The latter statement was important because it eventually allowed Barbara to effect a reconciliation with her mother by only hating what she did. The admission that she hated her mother was a spontaneous interpretation of her acid trip. In the original trip she was concerned with the bum acid that Sharon gave her. She was so angry she felt like strangling herself. But she did neither. She saw Frank (father) as "groovy" again, called Sharon (mother) a bitch, put down her mother, and then said, "I want to go to bed." In this way she gained her revenge but it was a nightmare. Frank confessed his love. She was afraid to believe it. She attempted to start a relationship with Barry, a straight (sexless) neighborhood boy, but it was not satisfying. She couldn't believe her father, she couldn't accept her mother. Sharon (her mother) was transformed into a lesbian and everyone—men and women alike—began having sexual relations with her (tearing off her clothes). Barbara was admitting her lesbian attraction to her mother for the first time. In later dreams she had actual lesbian experiences. The bum acid trip ended with the devils destroying the beauties of heaven, which represented her despair over ever effecting a reconciliation with God.

During this session she began indicating the tremendous number of men with whom she had slept. Her admission of the conflict between her mother and father and herself in the nightmare and the fact that it aroused homosexual and nymphomanic desires enabled her to discuss it outside the dream. She was able to recognize that she felt her parents would be relieved if she died— that "then she'd (the mother) never have to worry about my father leaving her for me." She felt that her mother would only love her if she gave up her father (a classical example of the Oedipal complex). Because Barbara won, she did not have to identify with the weaker mother, but at the same time, she lost her love.

Much of the material we covered to this point was highly significant. It dealt with Barbara's background and early experiences. The importance of these sessions was more meaningful to me and probably the reader than it was to Barbara—particularly on the conscious level. The goal during the initial stages of treatment, in addition to finding out who Barbara really was, was to prepare the unconscious for conscious insights. I was especially interested in connecting the influences of the past with those of the persent. To do this required a recitation of her more recent life. At first there were relatively few insights, but as time progressed, the connections were made.

The fifth interview brought to the fore the relationship between her lesbian tendencies and her feelings toward her mother and her sister. She describes the good mother (page 98) and then (page 101) she unconsciously associates the bountiful mother with the bountiful lesbians who panhandled just to succor her. She also has confused feelings for her mother and sister, who constitute a threat to steal her father's love. Barbara had previously caught her father doing to her mother what he did to her. And, he did the same thing to Marianne. Barbara is, of course, very hurt. She tries the same ploy as she did with mother, but in this case it's reality, not fantasy. Marianne responds to her sexual advances and Barbara is disgusted. Just as important is the fact that if daddy does it to Barbara, to mother, and to Marianne, he will do it to Holly. Barbara is petrified and fights tenaciously to keep her father for herself. Her fierce competitiveness is not confined to childhood but extends into adolescence and adulthood. She competes with Rozelle, who she sees as a sister, for her boyfriends. No wonder she felt so uncomfortable with women. They either aroused guilt, because they saw her for what she was, or they were a threat to her from a competitive standpoint.

Another part of Barbara's problem was her conflict with feelings of dependency.

In this same session Barbara began to understand her compulsion to tell all to anyone who would listen. She described Cindy "as a blabbermouth" who kept the secret (sort of) for many, many years. But she had to pay a price—she blabbed about everything else. And when she finally told her mother, she "blabbed" about her father, which is why she was able to talk about

A CASE HISTORY OF INCEST 217

incest in what appeared to be a calm manner during her first interview with me.

Throughout Barbara's story there are numerous reconfirmations of society's indifference to the "Silent Sin." Barbara told a teacher. She told her brother. She told Marianne, who told her father. She told Brian Reynolds and Jack Sanders guessed. Even Rozelle knew; it was so obvious. Yet no one did anything to stop it—not even Barbara's own mother. When her mother awoke from a sound sleep and went directly to the photos of Barbara and her father (page 143) it is obvious that she had prior knowledge of the pictures—pictures that were so abhorrent to her that she was able to completely repress the knowledge, which dramatically illustrates the power of the conscious mind to forget what it cannot accept. This same power enabled a mother to tolerate the silent sin. Later, when Barbara confronted her mother with the problem, her conscious mind was forced to acknowledge the existence of the photos which she then promptly destroyed.

In this session, too, Barbara's dependency conflict was illustrated again by her verbal disavowal of wanting something for nothing, yet accepting gifts and gratuities from all those who would provide them. Indirectly, through her feelings toward Rozelle, who was like a sister to her, she expressed her fear of being replaced by her sister and responded by taking away Rozelle's boyfriends. However, as soon as she unconsciously recognized the connection, she developed a headache and began resisting hypnosis. Barbara had always been afraid that Holly would displace her with her father but had yet to admit it. To do so would require that she reveal her true feelings about her father.

As therapy progressed, Barbara began to worry about what other people would think, which also suggested the embryonic formation of a conscience. She lied about Paul but later told the truth about Allan and Ronnie, and eventually about Paul. Her revelations also suggested that her mother abrogated her role as a mother by conferring the care of the house on her. Barbara even assumed the responsibility for rearing Holly. This confused Barbara because it is very difficult to be concomittantly a mother and a child.

On page 127 will be seen how Barbara subtly attempted to seduce me by relating how desperately she desired sexual relations. I declined her invitation by not responding. This reassured her. I also reassured her unconscious when I stated that her compulsive sex drive originated from her excitation in childhood by her father and therefore her behavior was understandable.

Barbara's description of her dual relationship with Allan and Ronnie (page 130) represented several important milestones in treatment. The first was that after having lied about it initially she was able to relate the truth despite it being "horribly embarrassing" to her. Curing the patient of lying is a vital element in the treatment of a psychopath, who is given to lying simply for the sake of lying. It is noteworthy that Barbara's confession immediately followed my unspoken refusal to accept her proposition and carried with it her admission that a fatherly transference, in the true sense of the word, was occurring. The second important element was my statement, "Because you were interested in it," in response to her question, "God, how could I do anything like that?" It was a very matter-of-fact comment. I was telling it "like it is," and at the same time communicating that I accepted it. Then, the third element appeared. For the first time Barbara was able to us a taboo word—taboo for her—to describe a highly personal and intimate behavior: "Allan was fucking me." It is essential to remember that although Barbara had used these words before, it had never been in reference to herself, always to someone else. This represented a further acceptance of self. Reassured of her self-worth, she was able to face the sexual act more directly.

Barbara's confusion (see pages 131-32) over her ambivalent feelings toward "Allan-the-pure" and "Ronnie-the-virile" is common to many women. Interestingly enough, faced with the choice, most women, while overtly praising the attributes of "Allan-the-pure," in the final analysis often choose "Ronnie-the-virile."

Her revelation (page 133) of the relationship with Allan and Ronnie also stimulated the insight that her mind was "going a mile a minute" during sexual relations.

An exceptional event occurred when Barbara, in the form of Cindy, relived the manner in which she revealed her sexual relationship with her father to her mother. The entire crux of therapy came into sharp focus when she said, (page 140), "Oh, my God! This didn't happen to Cindy! It happened to Barbara! It really happened to Barbara—to me!" Finally able to face the full brunt of her guilt, Barbara would no longer have to lie to herself. This was a major insight.

On the surface, it would seem that once Barbara had brought the entire affair into the open, her conflict would have disappeared. But her guilt was much deeper than that. In addition, there was also another conflict to be faced. Barbara had related (page 143) that her mother never blamed her for "having sex with the guys"; this made her feel unprotected because her mother was still basically unconcerned. Had the mother really been concerned, she would have put a stop to her promiscuity. That was what Barbara wanted. And, although her father spanked her, she was much more likely to interpret this as love than the mother's specious acceptance, which was really apathy and hence rejection.

The above revelations unlocked another compartment in a deeper level of Barbara's mind. She related a dream where "things" threatened her mother (Maxine, the beagle) the puppies (her brother and sister), and all the children from school. The things that no one can see (the Silent Sin) represented the unacknowledged incestuous relationship. Both daddy and Barbara concluded an unspoken covenant to leave Maxine (the mother) and her puppies (her siblings) to destruction by the "things." This allowed Barbara and her father to reserve the world for themselves—a virtual re-creation of the Garden of Eden.

Barbara's hostility to her mother had always been secreted from her consciousness but not so hidden that it could not be detected in its disguised from. Her hatred for her sister, who represented an even greater threat to her exclusive possession of the father, was even more repressed—perhaps it weighed on her like the mark of Cain.

Whether her guilt emanated from her present life, or from the collective unconscious as described by Jung, or yet again her soul, is a matter of conjecture and subject to individual interpretation. To Barbara, however, the idea of her God and her soul was very real, even though it was buried deep in her unconscious.

In her second interpretation of her nightmare, Barbara became even more aware of the mutual hatred that existed between her and her mother. In her first interpretation she killed her mother by leaving her to the mercy of the "things" outside the lighthouse. In the second interpretation, she perceived the mother seeking revenge by strangling her. But interestingly enough, even though the deepest layer of her unconscious deciphered the nightmare, the more conscious reaches of her mind were still unable to acknowledge her hostility toward the mother, as reflected by a subsequent statement (page 155), "But I know it was all in my dream—in the nightmare. She never felt that way about it really. Not really."

Barbara's flirtation with Scientology was stimulated by Walter and Sandy, but it also represented her attempt to be reconciled with God. Although pressure had been exerted by the members of this sect for her to terminate therapy, I was not overly concerned. I knew we were close to the end and that Barbara wanted to see it through. More importantly, Barbara stated that she thought God was within herself (page 162). The one thing I didn't want was to create a conflict within Barbara by dividing her loyalties between therapy and her religious beliefs. I offered no judgment about her affiliation and eventually, as I expected, completely disillusioned with Scientology, she terminated her membership.

From a professional standpoint, the successful treatment of Barbara, both as an individual and as a psychopathic personality, was a most rewarding experience. For Barbara there were many signs of cure by the end of our association. She was able to accept herself. She resolved many of her feelings toward her parents and sister. She stopped loving her father as a lover and began loving him as a father, which will enable her to form a relationship with a more suitable male than heretofore. Although she never acquired complete insight into her hostility toward her mother, much of it was drained away during the course of treatment. As a result, she will stop competing with the mother, thus permitting the relationship between father and mother to improve and which, in turn, will help the father feel more fatherly toward Barbara. She also began to see herself more positively as a woman, as reflected toward the end of therapy in her choice of more feminine clothes. This will, in the future, substantially reduce her homosexual tendencies.

Another sign of improvement was the definite cessation of her compulsive sexual activity. She also began to enjoy kissing, was able to achieve a climax, ceased lying, and, perhaps most important of all, was able to give up drugs.

In addition, her deep religious feelings became a source of comfort and love rather than a source of pain as her image of a wrathful, vengeful God changed.

All in all, for Barbara, life became worth living.

I am particularly pleased with marathon hypnotherapy as a tool in the treatment of the psychopath. As indicated earlier, the psychopath is ordinarily highly resistant to the usual techniques designed to alter his antisocial behavior. He is difficult to treat for two reasons: (1) Lack of a certain type of anxiety related to the absence of that part of the superego known as the conscience; and (2) lack of empathy and affinity for people, which is associated with the absence of another part of the superego known as the ego ideal. Consequently, the psychopath is unmotivated to change his behavior. He cannot be motivated by fear or anxiety because whatever fear or anxiety he suffers is only in immediate response to a particular situation. Remove the situation and you remove the fear. A person with a strong conscience, however, always carries the situation with him and hence the anxiety. This anxiety provides a constant source of motivation, which, in turn, creates the necessary conditions for a permanent change in behavior.

A person will also change his behavior to please someone for whom he has a deep affinity and respect. By incorporating the admired person's values into his own superego, he is provided with an additional source of permanent motivation. But the psychopath possesses neither of these incentives and therefore usually fails to profit from experience.

There is a way to treat a psychopath that takes these deficiencies into consideration. It involves effecting an intense transference reaction by a process I refer to as the arousal of existential anxiety through sensory deprivation. But it is akin to brainwashing and I hesitate to use it on moral grounds. In addition it is somewhat time-consuming and requires the therapist to have absolute legal and physical control over the patient, which is not likely to happen outside a maximum-security prison.

On the other hand, marathon hypnotherapy can be used in private practice. Its only drawback is that not everyone can be hypnotized.

Barbara, of course, had guilt and anxiety, but her guilt and anxiety mobilized self-destructive rather than constructive forces. The problem, therefore, was to eliminate the self-destructive types of guilt and anxieties and then to rebuild a healthier personality based on a less destructive type of anxiety or remnants of an ego ideal—if either could be found. Fortunately, there were two sources. One was an extremely deep and intense religious conviction that became increasingly apparent during the analysis of her dreams and LSD trips. The other was the love and true concern her father gave her prior to the initiation of the incestuous relationship.

The first step was to eliminate the malignant type of self-destructive anxiety. This was acomplished by Barbara reexperiencing each painful psychic episode from which the self-destructive type of anxiety emanated during hypnosis. However, when her psyche could not stand the conflicts even under hypnosis, she could relive the events by indirection through Cindy or through analyzing her own dreams.

Both of these devices, incidentally, were devised at this time to handle what appeared to be insurmountable barriers. Conducting the hypnotic session in a marathon fashion contributed to Barbara's cure by exhausting the emotional charges attached to her negative experiences. The marathon sessions facilitated deep and rapid insights by keeping her revelations of past and present events closely associated so that she could remember and relate them to one another with greater acumen.

And finally, hypnotic age-regression provided the means of activating benign forces of her pre-incest personality, which, in turn, provided the solid foundation for her present healthy personality. I doubt that this would have been possible under other conditions than hypnotic age-regression.

Barbara is now about 85 percent cured. The remainder of her cure, which consists mainly of the acquisition of more values from society, will come in the future—perhaps 10 percent within the next year, the rest within five years. Barbara will have certain advantages in resolving the problems of life. This is, in part, due to treatment because treatment made her irrational unconscious available to the reasonable conscious mind and her acceptance of self made her want to think reasonably. The average person does not have his unconscious motivations so available to his conscious processes. And since buried within the unconscious are the seeds of one's own destruction (sometimes referred to as the death wish by Menninger and Freud), the more a person knows about that province, the more he can control its influence.

Interestingly enough, having once been a psychopath is not without its rewards. It may have contributed to Barbara's charming, extroverted personality and her ability to handle herself adroitly in social situations. Moreover, Barbara has the advantage of certain innate characteristics: her superior intelligence, which, if measured, I would estimate would show an IQ close to 150; her physical appearance, which is quite attractive; and an enormous amount of energy.

Within the next year Barbara should begin forming healthier, more permanent relationships with responsible persons and in doing so, she will acquire their value systems. This will enable her to terminate the mutually exploitative types of relationships she had in the past in which everybody lost.

Barbara married in 1970 and at this moment is living happily in Farrell, in her own apartment several blocks from her parents' home. She has had a child and for the first time in her life she appears to have a completely compatible relationship with her mother and a normal, father-daughter relationship with Mr. Gale.